POLICY INTEGRATION IN CANADIAN AGRICULTURE

IOWA STATE UNIVERSITY CENTER FOR
AGRICULTURAL AND RURAL DEVELOPMENT

POLICY INTEGRATION IN CANADIAN AGRICULTURE

ROBERT W. CROWN

Associate in Economics; Program Specialist, Center for Agricultural and Rural Development, Iowa State University

EARL O. HEADY

C. F. Curtiss Distinguished Professor in Agriculture; Professor of Economics; Executive Director, Center for Agricultural and Rural Development, Iowa State University

THE IOWA STATE UNIVERSITY PRESS, AMES, IOWA

OTHER BOOK PUBLICATIONS of the Center for Agricultural and Rural Development are available as follows:

Size, Structure, and Future of Farms, 1972
Future Farm Programs: Comparative Costs and Consequences, 1972
Sociological Perspectives of Domestic Development, 1971
Benefits and Burdens of Rural Development: Some Public Policy Viewpoints, 1970
A North American Common Market, 1969
Food Goals, Future Structural Changes and Agricultural Policy: A National Basebook, 1969
Alternatives for Balancing World Food Production Needs, 1967
Roots of the Farm Problem, 1965
Economic Development of Agriculture, 1965
Family Mobility in our Dynamic Society, 1965
Farmers in the Market Economy, 1964
Our Changing Rural Society: Perspectives and Trends (developed by the Rural Sociological Society under editorship of James H. Copp), 1964
Adjustments in Agriculture—A National Basebook, 1961

Library of Congress Cataloging in Publication Data

Crown, Robert W. 1940–
Policy integration in Canadian agriculture.
Includes bibliographical references.
1. Agriculture and state—Canada.
2. Agriculture—Economic aspects—Canada.
I. Heady, Earl Orel, 1916–, joint author.
II. Title
HD1787 1972.C74 338.1′8′0971 78–171168
ISBN 0–8138–0275–X

Composed and printed by
The Iowa State University Press

First edition, 1972

CONTENTS

PREFACE

THE CANADIAN Federal Task Force on Agriculture recently released the results of its inquiry into the problems, policies, and programs for the Canadian agricultural sector.[1] Contact with the research behind the report began when the authors were employed by one of the contractors consulting with the Task Force during 1968 and 1969. Our employer was responsible for presenting an inquiry into the livestock, poultry, and feed grain economy—Task Force Project 3.[2] But during the course of the research it became increasingly difficult to confine our attention to that narrow commodity group, for we judged that (1) the real problems of the livestock and feed grains producer were not uniquely his by virtue of his specific enterprises and could not be properly treated using the commodities as instruments; (2) the diversity in livestock and feed grains production methods, volume of output, and the combination of these with other enterprises, both within and between regions, made livestock and feed grains not one economy, but many; and (3) major problems faced by livestock and feed grains producers resulted from the policies for and the actions of producers of other commodities in the same way that policies for and the actions of livestock and feed grains producers created problems for the producers of other commodities.

---

1. Federal Task Force on Agriculture, Canadian Agriculture in the Seventies (Ottawa: Queen's Printer, 1970).

2. Acres Research and Planning, "Problems, Policies, and Prospects for the Feedgrain-Livestock Economy," report to the Federal Task Force on Agriculture, 1969, vol. 1, 2, 3, 4. Available at the Canadian Dept. of Agr. Library, Ottawa.

We further judged that a similar set of considerations would best be taken into account when studies of single categories of agricultural inputs were undertaken. Our report to the Task Force contained some analysis of these considerations.

It is now very evident that we view the problems of Canadian agriculture (and probably agriculture in general) in a significantly different way than did the Task Force. Their approach, as revealed in their report, appears to emphasize continued use of commodity manipulation and the regulation of specific inputs as instruments of policy. By contrast, we would say that the total problem in agriculture is essentially different from the sum of the problems of commodities and inputs, and that the sum of all commodity- and input-oriented programs would probably not have the beneficial impact on incomes and farm welfare that programs designed for these specific problem areas could. It is possible that the Task Force was striving to demonstrate to policy makers a degree of political acceptability in their proposals by showing that no special interest group, however small and insignificant its voting power or economic contribution, had been left unconsulted. But in this effort the Task Force would have subjected themselves to the same kinds of diverse pressures with which government itself must continually contend. As a result the Task Force report tends to read as a list of the multidirectional urgings of the many rather than providing the basic reasoning which could generate an integrated, purposeful thrust of government leadership. Although the Task Force complains in the preface of its report that "few researchers associated with agriculture were willing to venture far from the status quo and make recommendations for startling changes in the industry," the Task Force itself shares its own criticism.

In this volume we have developed a noncommodity approach to agricultural policy, an approach suggested originally in our Task Force report. As we indicate in the text, most of the individual programs for individual commodities (a concern occupying fully half the Task Force's attention) can be made redundant if programs are developed and directed specifically at the income problems of commercial and noncommercial farmers, and if government provides an arena in which adjustment can proceed at sufficient speed to allow agriculture to provide adequate incomes for families remaining as active participants in the sector.

Wherever possible, we have tried to incorporate new ideas into existing institutions, rather than suggesting that current structures be destroyed and replaced with something novel. The latter scheme would, in effect, "throw out the baby with the bathwater," for many Canadian agricultural institutions can continue to play vital roles even though the roles may be modified versions of those accepted traditionally. In this way, concurrently with suggesting a more active leadership stance on government's part, we have attempted to capture genuine political acceptability by not challenging existing power structures.

We are fully aware that the speed of political life can force the evolution of government programs past the point at which they are discussed in a book or paper published at a fixed time. Such could well be the present case, for this book will probably be published after the specific programs alluded to have been modified. For example, in Canada, farm products marketing programs are scheduled for revision in late 1971, and a federal election may be called in early 1972 which could bring with it a spate of proposals for "new" farm programs. Yet this possibility in no way invalidates the discussion contained here, which is concerned with the direction of agricultural policy required to solve basic problems of farm and rural people, and some possible program types for the implementation of the policy. If programs exist, or are forthcoming, that capture the essence of the policy, then they could most certainly be retained in any set of specific new proposals.

Moreover, the logic and suggestions contained in the text have potential application in countries other than Canada. It would be a reasonably straightforward matter to rewrite the entire manuscript using another nation's institutions, programs, and policies as a base. The number of existing programs retained and the number that would be rejected in a final program of action would of course vary, but the basic analysis leading up to the final program would be the same.

Throughout our work, we benefited from contact with two groups of colleagues. The first includes the other members of the research team which prepared the report for the Task Force. They were Barry G. MacFarlane, Cesar J. Vanneste, John W. Knox, and Dr. E. L. Baum, who was in large measure responsible for the original conception of the study. The second group, at Ames, Iowa, includes Kenneth J. Nicol (M. Sc., University of Alberta), Craig V. Fulton (M. Sc., University of Manitoba), and Dr. A. Gordon Ball. One of the authors (Robert Crown) was also privileged to meet many ranking provincial government officials and leaders of farm organizations during the course of the original research for the Task Force. However, the errors, omissions, and conclusions are our own, and we accept the responsibility for them.

1 AN ANALYSIS OF THE PAST

1 Agricultural Policy's Drift into the 1970s

CANADIAN AGRICULTURAL POLICY has evolved over the years in response to the demands of farmers, agribusiness interests, consumers, and elements in the nonagricultural sectors wishing to use agriculture as a means to their own ends. The evolution has occurred in much the same way as the Canadian constitution—piecemeal, without an initial motivating impetus, and in response to the perceived needs of the day. One sees in Canada not an agricultural policy in the sense of a well-conceived, integrated thrust of action for the achievement of a predefined goal, but rather a set of actions taken to solve perceived problems of the moment. One does not see one agricultural policy, but many.

The truth of this situation was seen as long ago as 1946 by Cairnes and reaffirmed recently by McCalla and in the resolutions of the Agricultural Institute of Canada.[1] The reasons for such an evolution and an explanation of why the "policies" were formulated on behalf of the agricultural sector are the topics of Part 1 in this book. The reason for the piecemeal characteristic of the policy evolution or "drift," as we choose to call it, is both economic and political.

It is economic in the sense that people frequently do not assume high enough uncertainty levels or low enough discounting factors to future events when mak-

1. Articles by Andrew Cairnes, Agr. Inst. Rev. 1 (1946):539; A. F. McCalla, A Review and Appraisal of Agricultural Policies in Canada, a paper presented to the Canadian Agricultural Economics Society, Thirteenth Annual Workshop, Guelph, Ontario, 1968, p. 5; Agricultural Institute of Canada Resolution, Agr. Inst. Rev. 23 (1968):26-27.

ing a decision today to permit long-term benefits to outweigh short-term benefits. This attitude favoring short-run policies is reinforced by the political realities of Canadian agricultural policy making. At the micro, grassroots level, farmers have tended to see themselves as producers of specific commodities and to organize their political activities around a commodity or sets of commodities. But this natural affinity among producers of similar commodities prevents them from seeing that proper emphasis is placed on farm problems more fundamental than commodity problems.

When this commodity subdivision of the agricultural sector is further subdivided by province or region, whatever power farmers might have exercised for the attainment of policy goals as a unified force is scattered. The sum of the parts is much weaker politically than the whole could be. Furthermore, the emphasis in policy is much different than it could otherwise be. This is examined later in more detail.

Possibly these two factors could be "lived with," in that there might not be a real social cost involved, borne by farmers as human beings, in following policies resulting from the short-term and commodity-oriented approach to problems. This would be so if the sum of the effects of the short-term and commodity-oriented policies enacted over time actually solve the fundamental long-term problems of the sector.

But, as will be demonstrated in a subsequent chapter, the typical policy instruments used in Canada cannot be expected to solve agriculture's fundamental problems. However, because farm groups and politicians have presumed that the instruments could "work," attitudes have formed which tend to prevent a fundamental change in the agricultural policy structure; that is, a qualitative change in policy. Thus, in essence, we are faced today with a set of entrenched institutions and programs that have survived beyond the time when they were thought to be remedies for problems, in spite of doubt about their continued usefulness.

The rest of this chapter encapsulates the drift of policy making and institution creation to the present. It shows that the fundamental problems of Canadian agriculture have yet to be solved. This leads one to question why the policies have failed; and, assuming that the reasons for failure could have been known all along, why pressure has not been exerted for successful policies. Suggested answers to these questions follow.

EVOLUTION

Confederation to 1929. In pre-Confederation Canada and for a considerable period of time afterward, farming represented a way of life for most of Canada's population, providing an instant source of real income for new settlers and food for the growing towns. But as a drive for independent and viable nationhood took hold, overt policies directed toward the development and growth of the agricultural sector as an industry were instituted.[2]

As a matter of national policy, land was sold cheaply or even granted to willing settlers newly immigrated from Europe. Thus the two prime inputs in an initially subsistence agriculture—land and labor—were combined to provide a growing agricultural output. Complementary policies aimed at the expansion of agricultural output were instituted, such as government supported research, extension, and credit programs; subsidized transportation rates for prairie grain going for export; and political propagandizing about the value of the family farm. In Canada's early agricultural policy, in fact, one gets a preview of a policy prescription widely and correctly offered to emerging nations in the 1960s and 1970s; that is—build a solid agricultural sector as a necessary basis for an expanding industrial and urban economy.

These expansionary or developmental policies had the effect of enlarging the volume of output offered in the market, in contrast to compensation policies which mitigate the effects of adverse occurrences—

2. This section draws heavily on the keystone work of W. M. Drummond, W. J. Anderson, and T. C. Kerr, Review of Agricultural Policy in Canada (Ottawa: Agricultural Economic Research Council of Canada, June 1966). Their work draws together data from about 120 scattered sources and presents a history that anyone having access to their book would benefit from reading.

that is, welfare policy.[3] The expansionary policies were aimed in large measure at achieving the goals of national economic development, rather than at solving specific problems of low farm sector income, low prices, or resource immobility. This is evident if the prevailing national economic and political setting is considered.[4] One can safely hypothesize that eastern manufacturers would have been eager for expanding demand for manufactured products throughout the country. Hence they would encourage both expanding incomes in the farm sector and lower prices for agricultural products in the nonfarm sector, with the result that a larger part of consumers' incomes would be available to spend on manufactured goods.

These two ends were not essentially in conflict at that time, for farm income could rise by expanding output and reducing per unit costs by gaining benefits of scale economies, at the same time as per unit product prices were falling. This can be demonstrated by use of the following equation showing net farm income as a difference between total revenue and total cost:

$$NR = P_y \cdot Y - P_x \cdot X \qquad (1.1)$$

where

NR = net revenue
P_y = product price per unit
Y = number of units of output
P_x = input price per unit
X = number of units of inputs

If Y expands rapidly, and P_x declines as economies of scale are realized, P_y can fall and still result in a growth in NR. Hence it would be possible for both farm and nonfarm sectors to gain from the type of developmental policies instituted in Canada. Policies which encouraged both tendencies could yield a posi-

3. See Earl O. Heady, Agricultural Policy under Economic Development (Ames: Iowa State Univ. Press, 1962), Chap. 1.

4. Drummond, Anderson, and Kerr, Review of Agricultural Policy in Canada, pp. 68-69.

tive sum outcome for the well-being of all citizens.

It is interesting to observe that U.S. agricultural policy up to 1919 did not vary significantly from that in Canada. The only real difference seems to be that the Canadian Government was able to withstand farmers' demands for market price supports as an aid to growing net income while the U.S. Government began price support of various commodities as early as 1919.[5] As a demonstration of this resistance, in 1919 the Canadian Government suspended the operations of the Board of Grain Supervisors (a body charged with the orderly marketing of the 1917 and 1918 grain crops), instituted the Canada Wheat Board for the marketing of the 1919 crop, then suspended all active participation in marketing and merely set some ongoing rules of the game for the private trade. For the decade of the twenties, when U.S. farmers were relying on government payments and regulations to mitigate against the vagaries of commodity cycles, market pricing, and income fluctuation, Canadian farmers, particularly the western grain growers, were experimenting with producer cooperatives. By 1925, after five years of incorporation, cooperative wheat pools were marketing about 50 percent of the grain crop.[6]

This experience with grassroots self-help among farmers has left both positive and negative residuals for the policy maker of the 1970s. On the positive side, the farmers' discovery that they could help themselves has probably helped Canada keep free of the types of farm programs which have haunted the United States (such as extensive land banking, parity price formulas, and offices to purchase surplus commodities). On the negative side, however, the growth of self-help from the grassroots level upward has probably encouraged the approach to today's real farm problems on the regional, single-commodity level while clouding the recognition that some farm problems are both larger and more fundamental than those which can be solved

5. Heady, Agricultural Policy under Economic Development, pp. 26-31.

6. Drummond, Anderson, and Kerr, Review of Agricultural Policy in Canada, p. 30.

through commodity means, a point expanded in Chapter 3.

The Depression. The depression of the 1930s seemed to have special penalties for farm people. Between 1928 and 1933 net farm income in aggregate declined from $642 million to $109 million while physical output remained virtually constant. This is in part due to a growth in farm population over the same period as persons returned to the land when nonfarm employment became scarce. Nevertheless the success of the growth and development policies of the preceding decades left agriculture with expanded resources, debts, and capacity. With no alternative employment which would yield a better return, the resources committed to agriculture were used in agricultural production. But with declining nonfarm incomes, the effective demand for farm products declined, and with it, prices and total revenues.

The solution to the problem appeared to be in farmers raising the per unit price of commodities by withholding the commodities from markets. The reasoning might have run as follows: With a low price elasticity of demand for food, a reduction in the quantity of commodity offered for sale would raise the price per unit by a larger percentage than the percentage cutback. As a result total revenue would rise; and with no real increase in total costs, net revenue would improve. There might even be declining costs as less output was produced.

As will be shown in the following chapter, this could be a reasonable theory to employ as a basis for policy if it applies to the problem, and if the elasticities of demand and supply are of the right magnitudes. In the depression, however, the loss of purchasing power in the nonfarm sector had the effect of lowering aggregate effective demand at all prices—that is, there was a backward movement of the entire demand schedule. As a result the market withholding action could not effectively raise net revenues as hoped, even though per unit prices for some items could have been raised momentarily.

Buoyed by their successes with voluntary producer

cooperatives in the 1920s, and in spite of the failure of several cooperatives to receive legal sanction by being declared ultra vires in the Supreme Court of Canada, farmers pressed for federal legislation which would give them the power to form compulsory cooperatives. Such an act did not come, however, until 1934 when the National Products Marketing Act (NPMA) was passed. This act itself was declared ultra vires in 1935 on the grounds that it violated the sole right of provinces to regulate trade within their borders. (The various provincial schemes of the 1920s were declared ultra vires because they attempted to regulate interprovincial trade—a federal jurisdiction.) The initial passage of the NPMA, however, gave added encouragement to the movement for producer organized cooperatives. Within eighteen months of its passage and before it could be found unconstitutional, twenty-two cooperatives were planned and nineteen were in operation. After the ruling on the NPMA and its acceptance by the federal government in 1937, most provinces reenacted legislation giving producers the power to form voluntary cooperatives on a strictly provincial basis.

It has been suggested that the enactment of the NPMA was less a response to the pressure of the depression than a logical culmination of the attitudes developed during the 1920s.[7] As such it does not rank high as a relief measure.

The major federal move for the assistance of agriculture came to the assistance of prairie grain growers. The initial assistance came during 1930 when world grain markets were in a serious decline. It came in the form of help for the pool companies, which had been formed in the 1920s as voluntary corporations. In its first overt act for over a decade, the federal government organized the Central Selling Agency for the Pools, and appointed a federally paid general manager. The agency was empowered to purchase Canadian grain when world prices were low, hold it, and sell it when world prices rose. There was no guarantee that the gambles the agency took would yield higher prices,

7. Ibid., p. 36.

although they appeared to do so, and there was no compensation for farmers if gambles failed.[8]

This policy lasted five years until 1935 when the Canada Wheat Board was reestablished. The board was charged with the responsibility of maintaining a floor price for western grain. Farmers could either sell to the board or sell it in the open market. Initially the board offered 87.5 cents for "No. 1 Northern" wheat (the benchmark commodity) at Fort William, to be paid if the free market price fell to 90 cents per bushel. But the free market price was well in excess of 90 cents for most of 1936 and 1937. When prices fell to a level where board operations would be demanded, the board lowered its purchase price to 80 cents per bushel (1938-39). In 1939 the federal government, believing that the crisis of the thirties was over, decided to close the board once again.[9] This time, however, the wishes of the farm community prevailed and the board was retained. But board operations were largely curtailed after 1940 until the postwar days.

The government, not anxious to become permanently involved in agriculture, encouraged the impression that the various grain assistance policies were its response to a short-run emergency. One should note that Canadian wheat as an export commodity had been under pressure in world markets since 1917-18. European recovery after World War I seriously cut demand for imported grain at the same time as Canadian developmental policies, such as the expansion of acreage and productivity, added to supply and supply potential. It is reasonable to assume, as has been done, that even without the depression, the problem of western grain would have emerged during the thirties, and that some government action would have been demanded.[10] The advent of World War II served as a temporary solution to both problems of the 1930s, but with the end of the war (and to the present), the grain problems experienced during the depression remained.

By the beginning of the depression, farm debt in

8. Ibid., p. 38.
9. Ibid., p. 39.
10. Ibid., p. 37.

Canada was large. Much of the debt centered in the Prairie Provinces, where additions to fixed capital had appeared profitable during World War I and the 1920s. With the reduction of farm incomes in the 1930s the ability of farmers to service their debts declined. Foreclosure threats multiplied and various provincial and federal schemes were introduced to alleviate the problem. Most unserviced farm debt outside the Prairie Provinces was handled through the all-inclusive Mortgagor's and Purchaser's Relief Program which sought to effect voluntary reductions in debt through the consent of debt-holders. These were largely successful and required virtually no government money to administer.

Prairie farmers were given special consideration under the Debt Adjustment Board Program, which originally sought to find compromise arrangements, but which had to be reinforced by provincial and federal legislation. In 1934 the Farm Creditors' Act created boards of review with the power to enforce debt reduction if volunteer agreements failed. The estimated reduction of farm debt as a result of the 1934 act was about $54 million out of $158 million outstanding, affecting about thirty-two thousand farm families.[11] Once again, the prairie debt adjustment programs cost virtually nothing, but had the effect of keeping many farms in operation. It would be heartless to suggest that the farm families so bankrupted by the events of the depression ought to have been evicted. Nevertheless the program instituted did not get directly to the cause of the farm overcapacity problem. One could, for example, have designed a program in which farms about to be foreclosed fell to the government, which undertook to service the debt and rent the land to the incumbent farmer at whatever he could pay until he decided to move off—presumably when the urban job market opened up again. Thus the program merely postponed the day when adjustment would have to be made in the agricultural sector, giving the impression that the family farm was essentially desirable time to solidify into

11. Ibid., p. 40.

dogma, and convincing further generations to commit themselves to a less-than-secure future in farming.

Simultaneously with the depression, but not because of it, Canada became aware that her western settlement patterns and land-use methods were developed in ignorance of the ecological balance of the prairie. The upshot was prolonged drought during the thirties, resulting in demands for better soil management and conservation. The Prairie Farm Rehabilitation Act (PFRA) of 1935 sought to improve land use through the spread of research findings and financial support. However good the intentions of this program, the mode of implementation and its subsequent development tended to contribute to growing supply capacity and the weakening of markets as a provider of adequate farm incomes.

The Prairie Farm Rehabilitation Act disseminated information on a farm-to-farm basis, with the effect that the land became more productive per acre. The program sought to develop water resources, efficient utilization of marginal land, and the knowledge of soil structure and properties which could be used in improved fertilization. Later, PFRA undertook administration of resettlement programs and development of new farm areas.

Closely related to the PFRA was a program for the assistance of marginal-income farmers in time of crop failures. The Prairie Farm Assistance Act of 1939 undertook a kind of crop insurance for farms in marginal land areas. As such it kept farms operating in areas where agriculture held only a second order advantage and where nonuse of land would have been the best use of land. Hence, PFRA applied developmental impetus at a time when and in commodities for which restraint was required; and again it set up forces to counter those forces spurring natural adjustment of agriculture.

The depression dramatized the need for assistance in Canadian agriculture, just as it dramatized the need for stabilization and income policies in the nonfarm sector. But the instruments used to implement the policies contained very strong developmental elements.

None carried true compensation elements, even though the terms and language employed sounded as if income support would be the result of the programs. The significance for the modern policy maker of these initial attempts at "compensation" is that the labels, intentions, and the realities were confused. It was apparently not recognized at the time that the policy to support income (compensate) by restraining the flow of goods to market was in effect a developmental instrument, an attempt to raise output prices which, if successful, would call forth more output or more regulations; that a guaranteed floor price insured greater production, since output prices would be fixed with certainty, hence riskless; and that debt reduction and efficient land-use programs on the per farm level added to capacity, reducing the effective short-run cost of operation and enlarging efficiency and scale. The policies were called income maintenance policies, were intended as compensation policies, and in reality and effect were developmental.

World War II. If the policies implemented in the 1930s failed to solve the problem of low incomes in the farm sector, the mistake was fortuitous, for the demands placed upon the sector during World War II required not only the full capacity of agriculture as it was in 1939, but added capacity. As in the case of the days of national consolidation, the agricultural sector became an instrument serving national policy objectives, not only objectives of the sector itself.

The demands of the war fell roughly on the livestock industries, and the demand for grain, particularly as an export item, fell. In the grain-growing prairies the demand swung toward coarse grains and feed for the livestock industries. As a wartime precaution against inflation, the market prices of livestock items were roughly pegged, yet the Canada Wheat Board established floor prices for western grain. With free market prices naturalized as an adjustment mechanism, explicit policies were developed to facilitate the change in production patterns.

The goal of greater livestock output was sought by the implementation of the Feed Freight Assistance Act of 1941, in which the government paid all or part of the cost of transporting western feed grains and millfeeds from Thunder Bay, Ontario (the Lakehead) to various destination points and elevators in eastern Canada. The subsidy also covered the movement of grains to British Columbia. In this total support package were included subsidies for elevator storage costs in the east and at the Lakehead, assistance to the processors of feed, and subsidies to cover the cost of storage of grain shipped from the Prairie Provinces early in the summer.[12] In addition to this act, subsidies were instituted to reward the production of grade A hogs (Canadian bacon hogs), hogs whose superior quality could not be reflected in higher market prices.

On the other hand, food grain stocks increased in 1940 and 1941 as a result of good crops in 1939 and a decline in foreign trade. Whereas the Canada Wheat Board served as a voluntary alternate market for grain during the 1930s, it was eventually made the sole legal purchaser and seller of wheat in 1943. The Minister of Trade and Commerce of the day declared:

> By placing control of the purchase and sale of Canadian wheat in the hands of the Wheat Board it will be possible to deal with current and future marketing problems on a basis more suitable to war conditions.[13]

This development had been urged by the farm community during the 1930s and was adopted only when it served the needs of the nation as a whole.

In addition to compulsory wheat marketing through the Board, the years 1940 and 1941 saw the first acreage quotas enforced for wheat growers. This did not mean that they were enjoined from growing coarse grain, however. In fact to encourage a switch to

---

12. For a complete description and analysis of the Feed Freight Assistance Act see T. C. Kerr, An Economic Analysis of the Feed Freight Assistance Policy (Ottawa: Agricultural Economic Research Council of Canada, 1966).

13. Drummond, Anderson, and Kerr, Review of Agricultural Policy in Canada, p. 54.

coarse grain production, high initial cash payments were offered for coarse grain deliveries, subsidies were offered for lime and fertilizer, and the Feed Freight Assistance Act gave a favorable outlook to demand.

Canadian agriculture responded well to the developmental policies of the war. A proliferation of subsidies, which grew as the war continued, raised the effective farm price of selected commodities, lowered the effective farm prices of inputs and services used in the production of "desirable" commodities, and provided stimulation to output in the absence of rising market prices. Unfortunately for the modern policy maker, the success of the wartime policy mix has been remembered, but the specific circumstances for which the mix was desirable and successful have tended to fade. As a consequence many wartime emergency policies have become institutionalized, and with few exceptions (e.g., hog premiums), remain today. Subsidies remain on various inputs and outputs, and the Wheat Board has remained, by and large, the sole purchaser and seller of wheat and coarse grains. Because the instruments were successful in attaining one set of goals, many have come to assume that the same set of policy instruments will be successful in attaining the goals of the 1970s.

Transition to Peacetime. The problems of transition from a wartime to a peacetime economy in Canada were anticipated by the federal government as early as 1941, when it established the Advisory Committee on Reconstruction. The committee had five subcommittees, one of which studied agricultural reconstruction.

The philosophy of the day, as revealed in the report of the committee, was in general that the rehabilitation and development of the agricultural industry should not be considered as being distinct from that of the economy at large, in either the economic rationale governing the sector, or in the desires and goals of those within the sector. There were, admittedly, special problems resulting from the nature of agricultural production, from the existence of rural fundamental notions and from atomistic competition in agriculture, which warranted special attention; but essentially the sector should behave as all other sectors behaved.[14]

The committee report also revealed several commitments which the federal government sought to express as policies.[15] First, the government felt the moral obligation to prevent agricultural incomes from falling in any postwar slump. Secondly, the government was determined to prevent a repetition of (a) the failures of the soldier demobilization and settlement efforts which followed World War I, (b) the spread of bankruptcy and overpowering debt which had followed the expansion during World War I, and (c) the development of war-induced inflation.

Of prime importance here is the attack made to prevent falling farm incomes through the Agricultural Price Support Act of 1944. The act was designed ". . . for the support of prices of agricultural products during the transition from war to peace."[16] The government established a Price Support Board empowered to buy and sell agricultural commodities when market prices deviated from an ideal price which had been set through an averaging formula. It acted in the role of an office to purchase, and it appears to have incorporated ideas prevalent in the United States, notably the concept of parity achieved through the operation of an ever normal granary. Supplemental legislation in 1944 (the Export Credit Insurance Act) and 1947 (the Agricultural Products Act) was designed to increase foreign demand for Canadian agricultural products and to assist exportation, and the Canada Wheat Board became the sole seller of oats and barley in foreign markets in 1948.

14. The reliance on the price mechanism subject to stabilization as the force motivating and transferring wealth and welfare to the farm sector was the key mechanism in postwar adjustment. Drummond, Anderson, and Kerr, Review of Agricultural Policy in Canada, p. 55; and G. E. Britnell and V. C. Fowke, Canadian Agriculture in War and Peace, 1935-50, Food Res. Inst. (Stanford, Cal.: Stanford Univ. Press, 1962).

15. Drummond, Anderson, and Kerr, Review of Agricultural Policy in Canada, p. 56.

16. Quoted from Britnell and Fowke, Canadian Agriculture in War and Peace.

Domestically, the Agricultural Products Marketing Act (1949) allowed for cooperation between federal and provincial governments in finding improved methods of marketing, in addition to giving producer groups power over intraprovincial trade in agricultural commodities.

However, it is clear that all this activity centered on price supporting or stabilization;[17] and as will be shown in the following chapter the use of price mechanisms to support or stabilize net incomes was bound to be ineffective. In fact, the postwar transition to a peacetime economy demonstrated this inadequacy, as farm income did fall after the war, in real terms relative to prices of inputs. (Table 1.4 shows that while cash receipts tended to rise after 1949, operating expenses rose at a more rapid rate, putting pressure on net income.)

1950 to the Present. In spite of the failure of the price supportive measures implemented in the immediate postwar period to maintain current net farm incomes, the instruments employed over the past twenty years played only variations on the immediate postwar themes.

Subsidies on Inputs and Output. The belief that price support and stabilization automatically lead to improved farm incomes is demonstrated in Canada's Agricultural Stabilization Act. Written in 1958, this act incorporated the price support concept originally put forward in the Agricultural Price Support Act (1944) and gave the added responsibility of price stabilization to a newly constituted Price Support Board. The Agricultural Stabilization Act followed desires in the farm community for a firmer basis to price support. The Price Support Board of the earlier years had been cautious in its use of price supports, seldom exceeding 80 percent of the average price as a floor price, and supporting commodities only in "emergency" situations. The new board was directed to support nine named commodities at levels at least as high as 80 percent of the average of the past ten-year period.

17. This is also a conclusion in Drummond, Anderson, and Kerr, Review of Agricultural Policy in Canada, p. 55.

The board was further directed to limit total payments to individual producers in the belief that this would bias the program in favor of poorer producers, the smaller farmers.[18] It continues to function today.

In 1967 a Federal Dairy Commission was established whose goal was to support the incomes of nonfluid milk producers too poor to get contracts with various provincial milk marketing boards. This was done through the payment of subsidies for butterfat. Other instruments have attempted to stabilize income by neutralizing the effects of weather, commodity cycles, and other exogenous shocks. The order of magnitude of these expenditures is given in Table 1.1.

Within the general category of actions aimed at maintaining prices at given levels falls the entire cross section of producer marketing boards. Although these are producer boards whose expressed aim is to "market in an orderly fashion," the compulsory nature of most, and their activities in quota administration (to restrict supply) as well as promotion (to increase demand) have strong price manipulative overtones.

Finally, the Canada Wheat Board, the main element in Canada's marketing policy, acts as a compulsory producer marketing board. The board administers quotas (delivery and acreage); is the sole purchaser and seller of prairie grain (wheat, oats, and barley); sets pooled prices; and distributes special subsidies and payments. These activities have a strong price orientation, as opposed to income orientation.

A recent activity of the board has been the administration of Canada's Lower Inventories for Tomorrow (LIFT) Program: an attempt to withdraw acreage from production to help reduce the surpluses that have accumulated. This is not strictly a price supportive policy, but rather a program required to mitigate the effects of the board's paying prices which did not adequately reflect world demand for Canadian grain in light of existing stocks on hand.

Because of Canada's considerable dependence on the sale of grain both in world and domestic markets

18. Drummond, Anderson, and Kerr, Review of Agricultural Policy in Canada, p. 61.

Table 1.1. Expenditures by Federal and Provincial Governments on Agriculture, 1966-67

	Provincial	Federal ($ million)	Total	Percentage of Total
1. Production assistance				
Livestock	5.32	19.94	25.26	...
Crops	9.06	4.42	13.48	...
Land and water development	43.13	32.62	75.75	...
Farm credit	11.60	6.01	17.61	...
Other	3.08	1.58	4.66	...
Subtotal	72.19	64.57	136.76	31.0
2. Marketing assistance				
General	0.99	1.24	2.23	...
Livestock and products	3.52	9.12	12.64	...
Other	2.56	2.28	4.54	...
Subtotal	7.07	12.62	19.69	4.5
3. Price support and income assistance				
Agricultural state legislation board	...	96.21	96.21	...
Canadian dairy commission	...	0.04	0.04	...
Dairy products subsidy	13.68	...	13.68	...
Crop insurance (including PFAA)	0.84	2.18	3.02	...
Feed grain subsidy	...	21.17	21.17	...
Wheat storage	...	24.29	24.29	...
Adverse weather assistance	7.66	10.64	18.30	...
Crop and livestock compensation	0.09	1.32	1.41	...
Other	2.22	...	2.22	...
Subtotal	24.48	155.85	180.33	40.5
4. Extension	20.52	0.81	21.33	4.5
5. Research	12.76	46.48	59.24	13.5
6. Education	8.50	0.12	8.62	2.0
7. Other	12.41	3.79	16.20	4.0
Total	157.91	284.14	442.05	100.0

Source: S. W. Garland and S. C. Hudson, Government Involvement in Agriculture, a Report to the Federal Task Force on Agriculture, (Ottawa: Queen's Printer, 1968).

as a source of personal incomes, and the great distances that the grain must travel before being consigned to bottoms, two special forms of marketing assistance have evolved, the values of which are included in Table 1.1. The Crow's Nest Rail Rates have been a subsidized and hence reduced set of rail rates in effect since the turn of the century. As mentioned earlier, Feed Freight Assistance began during World War II as a stimulation to eastern livestock production. Currently the Feed Freight Assistance Program has become "a [policy] means in search of an end."

As in the case of the LIFT Program, the transportation subsidies are not price supports, but rather fall into a category of supports related to inputs and services used by farmers.

Growing Productivity. The second broad theme of Canadian policy that has survived since World War II is the belief that, in itself, increased production efficiency will lead to increased net farm incomes. As indicated in Table 1.1, many programs aimed at improved production techniques and their spread are currently under way.

In 1961-62 an initial and significant step was taken by the federal and provincial governments in concert to rationalize agricultural policy in Canada—the passing of the Agricultural Rehabilitation and Development Act (ARDA), which was later renamed the Agricultural and Rural Development Act in the second agreement in 1966. The program requires provincial initiatives in the attack on rural poverty, through provincial planning and programs best suited to the particular characteristics of the provinces, while financial underwriting by the federal government through the Department of Regional Economic Expansion (DREE) makes projects possible.

Initially, in 1961-62, ARDA followed programs similar to those of PFRA, in that emphasis tended to be on conservation and soil use—efficient land management on the national level. Clearly this approach had little to do with the root of rural and farm poverty—that is, the inability of resources, in spite of their most efficient combination, to produce enough, cheaply enough, to support a viable enterprise. Initial comments on the effectiveness of ARDA have been harsh, accusing the program of being too institutionally committed to the original PFRA type of program, and too small an effort in relation to the magnitude of the rural poverty problem.[19] However, all critics are careful to point out that insufficient observations have been made for conclusive judgments; and that the policy at least is concerned not so much with the parity of incomes between the farm and nonfarm sectors, as with income distribution within the farm sector.

More will be said in Part 2 about the kind of policy directions which could evolve out of the programs like ARDA, Area Development Act (ADA), and Fund for Regional Economic Development (FRED), and which could fully rationalize Canadian agricultural policy. For now we can see the predominance of price supportive and production-oriented programs as shown by the relative share of federal and provincial funds spent on the agriculture they command (Table 1.1).

Two additional attempts have been made to alleviate the problems of low incomes in agriculture. These have been broader programs, less specifically aimed at agriculture, and more concerned with the development of entire regional economies. Naturally if the programs generated under ADA and FRED were successful in creating secondary employment opportunities in various regions, then the agriculture of those regions could benefit. For this reason alone the programs' elements could profitably be retained in any new policy direction for Canada.

These two programs, like so many other attempts to improve farm income situations, offer only indirect help (necessary as they may be in setting up a favorable environment for the solution to agriculture's problem). Because they deal with specified project regions, ADA and FRED efforts could eliminate aid to persons in need of specific help not living in the region. Furthermore, ADA and FRED programs would tend to most benefit those in agriculture who are most capable of out-migration even without the programs. Such pro-

19. A. F. McCalla, Appraisal of Agricultural Policies in Canada, p. 14.

grams generally do not reduce or eliminate in-sector barriers to resource mobility, nor ease the difficulties encountered in out-migration from agriculture.

CANADA'S AGRICULTURAL PROBLEM REMAINS

One cannot doubt the sincerity of the men who asked for, and those who granted, the set of policy instruments with which Canadian agriculture is now encumbered. Clearly they asked for the programs which appeared to attack the problems as they were perceived: low prices and incomes, the uncertainty of the price and quantity of agricultural products, the impotence of the many small producers in the face of the few powerful buyers of produce and sellers of inputs, the alarming stability of farm prices concurrent with growth in the prices of purchased items, and the persistent flow of new techniques and machinery, all apparently vital for the survival of the farm, and all involving added investment and specialization. But, because the programs attempted to deal with each apparent problem as if it were unique and independent of all others, policy instruments have evolved which attempt to treat the symptoms of more fundamental problems rather than the root problems themselves.

In fact we see only two fundamental and interrelated problems confronting the agricultural sector and suggest that all other problems derive from these two. The first reflects the problem of the agricultural sector as a whole: when faced with national economic growth and development, the sectoral resource-use pattern cannot change as rapidly as the changing structure of relative factor prices, with the result that the sector as a whole operates in a suboptimal state. This problem is referred to as the adjustment problem and is discussed directly. The second problem is that of the distribution of income within the agricultural sector, the problem arising when exogenous technological changes appear and do not benefit all equally or positively. This problem is not ameliorated by the functioning of the price system; rather, the price system tends to exaggerate the problem. On the national level, there is a second income distribution problem: that is, the problem of a fall in the share of national income accruing to the agricultural sector as economic growth proceeds. This is in reality an extension of the adjustment problem, but we will consider it in the general discussion of the distribution problem for now.

Adjustment Problem. Three major kinds of economic change have occurred in Canada's agricultural sector in the past decade: changes in the prices of production inputs relative to each other; changes in the productivity of resources employed through technological innovation; and changes in per unit costs, per unit returns, and declining margins, as a result of nonfarm sector economic development.

From 1956 to January 1968, unit labor costs in Canadian agriculture increased by 80 percent, unit machinery costs rose by 24 percent, and unit fertilizer costs increased 22 percent.[20] This means that labor costs have grown relative to capital items by 31 percent and relative to fertilizers by 33 percent between 1956 and 1968, giving farmers added incentives to substitute other inputs for labor. Farmers have generally responded to the incentives, for they have attempted to reduce operating costs by substituting capital and other factors of production purchased from the nonfarm sector for labor.

The index of labor employment has declined to about 60 percent of 1950 levels, representing an average annual decline of about 3.3 percent. At the same time, the input of machinery, fertilizer, and real estate has increased substantially. (See Table 1.2.)

The shift in the mix of production inputs indicates that one form of rational adjustment has occurred in the farm sector—an increase in the use of less expensive inputs relative to the more expensive inputs. Yet the modest decline in the total amount of resources employed shows that the retirement of the more expensive inputs (labor) has not proceeded much faster than the rate at which the new inputs were being added.

20. Dominion Bureau of Statistics, Price Index of Commodities and Services Used by Farmers, Canada, Ottawa; D.B.S., Industrial Selling Price Index, 1956 = 100, Ottawa.

Table 1.2. Indexes of Inputs, Output, and Productivity by Categories of Input, Selected Years 1950-69 (1949 = 100)

	1950-54	1955-59	1960-64	1965-69	Annual Growth Rate since 1950 (%)
Inputs					
Real estate[a]	99	105	112	114	+1.0
Labor[b]	85	70	61	52	—3.3
Capital items (total)	108	124	139	170	+3.1
Machinery[c]	115	123	124	146	+1.5
Seed and feed	95	123	142	183	+4.5
Fertilizer	107	116	174	289	+8.8
Other[d]	110	131	160	181	+3.5
All inputs	95	94	96	101	+0.4
Output	120	127	141	169	+2.3
Productivity	126	135	147	167	+1.9

Source: Compiled from I. F. Furniss, Agricultural Productivity in Canada: Two Decades of Gains, Can. Farm Econ., Canadian Dept. of Agr., December 1970, pp. 16-27.

[a]Includes interest, depreciation and repairs on buildings, and property taxes on both owned and rented real estate.

[b]Includes operator, hired, and unpaid family labor.

[c]Includes fuel and other purchased items associated with machinery operation, plus interest and depreciation.

[d]Includes electric power, interest on investment in livestock, and purchased livestock, pesticides, breeding fees, etc.

Thus, even though the growth in nonfarm opportunities has drawn away much of the agricultural labor force, enough remains to produce a growing volume of output, about 2.3 percent growth per year since 1950.

What is more important is that the growth in productivity per unit of input (not just growth in the amount of output) shows that the new combinations of labor and purchased inputs are even more productive than the old; that is, the recombination of inputs has yielded an economy of scale, which is evidence of technological change in the farm sector. Without this, we would expect to see constant productivity ratios over time; instead, Table 1.2 shows an average annual growth in productivity of 1.9 percent since 1950.

Yet, in the course of economic development, the income and price elasticities of demand for foods and

Table 1.3. Canadian Income Elasticities for Selected Food Products

Product	Income Elasticity
Cereals	−0.5
Meat	+0.29
Milk	−0.02
Fats and oils	−0.07
Calories	+0.00
Proteins	+0.02
Animal products	+0.07

Source: Food and Agriculture Organization, Agricultural Commodities Projections to 1975, 1985, Rome 1967.

agricultural commodities tend to decline as these commodities assume positions of decreasing importance in family budgets (Table 1.3). Hence, the growing output of the agricultural sector earns less total income for the sector as time passes. Costs, on the other hand, tend to be determined for the farm sector by the alternate employment available for resources in the nonfarm sector. With economic process these determinations become more plentiful, and resource prices tend to rise accordingly.

Even with technological adjustments and adjustment in the resource mix in production, margins between per unit costs and per unit returns have declined steadily since 1949. Table 1.4 shows the changes in the ratio of farm receipts from the sale of agricultural products to total operating cost and depreciation for the years 1949 through 1969. (These operating costs include interest payments on indebtedness; presumably mortgages are a large part of this. In some economists' view, a farm enterprise should be charged on the basis of the opportunity cost of the land resource rather than on the contract price—that is, the amount of the mortgage. If this approach had been taken, the ratio may well have become less than unity, particularly since demand for land in most parts of Canada has generally doubled land prices in the past five to seven years.) A ratio equal to unity would indicate that farm cash receipts are just equal to operating expenses and depreciation, and that returns to operator labor, owners' equity, and management would be zero. Conceptually, the ratio measures the margin of

Table 1.4. Ratio of Receipts to Expenses, 1949-69 Selected Years

	Cash Receipts[a] ($ billion)	Operating Expenses and Depreciation[b] ($ billion)	Ratio
1949	2.4	1.2	1.98
1950	2.1	1.3	1.61
1951	2.7	1.5	1.88
1956	2.5	1.7	1.52
1957	2.5	1.7	1.51
1958	2.8	1.8	1.56
1964	3.5	2.5	1.39
1965	3.8	2.7	1.40
1966	4.2	3.0	1.43
1967	4.4	3.2	1.38
1968	4.4	3.4	1.30
1969	4.2	3.4	1.23

Sources: Dominion Bureau of Statistics, Farm Net Income, Catalogue No. 21-201 and 21-501, Ottawa; Farm Cash Receipts, Catalogue No. 21-001, Ottawa.

[a]Cash receipts include only monies received for produce sold, and exclude income in kind and government transfer payments.

[b]Operating expenses include taxes, interest on indebtedness, wages for hired labor and purchased inputs like fertilizers, seed, and machinery, but exclude a return to equity management or operator labor.

return over cost for a general unit of agricultural production. It is likely that farmers may try to select enterprises which have relatively larger margins (assuming they can be flexible) so that the "general unit of agricultural production" is a variable unit. No special significance is attached to year-to-year changes in the ratio; only the longer-term tendency is significant since it shows that agricultural enterprises in aggregate tend to experience shrinking margins.

In these circumstances, individuals generally attempt to "get ahead of the system" by adopting techniques, resource mixes, and product mixes that embody the most advanced knowledge available to the sector. Since these gains were to be had by specializing, many have done so and have constructed large scale, capital-intensive operations. This in turn means that once resources are employed in the specific agricultural activity they become fixed in the sense that they have little or no salvage value in other enterprises, farms, or sectors. In an attempt to gain in the face of changing market conditions, farmers have been forced to sacrifice resource mobility.

The nature of the adjustment problem and its economic content thus becomes clear. In short that which is lauded as progress on the national scale leads to the greater problem of the lack of resource mobility in the agricultural sector, and to the inability of the agricultural sector, unassisted, to rationalize its size, composition, and structure, under internal economic motives of profit maximization. It is just those motives which create the problem; they cannot also solve it.

With commodity and resource markets as they currently function, or as they might function under a changed policy regime, time alone will not solve the adjustment problem at an acceptable minimum cost to those farm families involved. What is required is a new set of government initiatives directed specifically at the problem.

For those with high sales volumes now, the adjustment problem is probably not critical, for they will likely remain in agriculture and grow if given only minimal encouragement. But for the farmers whose sales volume is less than $10,000, for example, the likely trends in economic factors and their ability to adjust to changes in economic factors will probably make adjustment more difficult as time proceeds.

The age distribution of farm operators whose sales volume is less than $10,000 is skewed toward the forty-five-years-and-older class. These persons are less able to migrate and probably less willing to make the investments necessary to grow.

But even immobility due to age might not be seen as critical if one could predict that the tendencies in postwar agriculture would change direction. However, one cannot make such a prediction. These tendencies are likely to persist under the stimulus of continued economic development of the nonfarm sector, the competitive character of the farm sector and individual income strategies, the decline in profit margins, and continued demand for research into agricultural production patterns.

There is little reason to believe that trends in prices of production inputs will not continue to encourage substitution of machinery, fertilizer, and land for labor. The price the farm sector must pay for the labor it requires is ultimately determined by the nonfarm price for the same quality of labor. This latter price will continue to rise.

By contrast, the cost of machinery, fertilizers, and other purchased inputs originating in the nonfarm sector will undoubtedly continue to decline relative to the price of labor. Reasonable degrees of competition—perhaps in the form of quality changes, service after sale, guarantees, and more convenient payment plans—between companies selling nonfarm inputs, should be sufficient to insure that increases in nonfarm productivity are passed on to the agricultural sector in the form of reduced real cost. This tendency is expected to accelerate as trade between Canada and the United States becomes freer. Undoubtedly farmers will take advantage of the changes in the relative prices of inputs.

Farmers, more than producers in any other sector, are price takers. If prices are low, a farmer can reduce output. But as an independent operator he would, in fact, merely sell less at the lower price. So his usual strategy for solving an unfavorable price and income situation is to produce more by employing new technology and/or increasing farm size in the hope of realizing scale economies and lower average costs. However, if a large number of farm operators use the same strategy, then the result is greater output in aggregate. Since aggregate demand is inelastic, an even greater decline in product price occurs.

Although today's individual farmer knows that his personal income-maximizing strategy will eventually be ineffective when other farmers follow his strategy, he cannot employ a different plan and be as well off as before (assuming he wishes to remain in agriculture). So, to obtain as large a share of sectoral income as he can, his best plan is to increase output and employ more new technology wherever possible. The result of all individuals following the "best" strategy means an increase in agricultural productivity, which leads to reduction of the number of farms and the size of the farm labor force when noncompetitive farmers retire from full-time farming.

As a result of pressures from farm groups and academics alike, it will likely continue to be federal and provincial government policy to undertake, or at least to provide assistance for, research into production and marketing problems. Thus, new technologies will continue to be developed. It is also likely that information on new methods, breeds, and crop varieties will continue to be disseminated through improved agricultural representative and educational services sponsored by the government. In fact, even with the government performing these services, private consulting firms have found it profitable to advise individual farmers and ranchers on problems of production and organizations. Finally, farmers and ranchers view themselves as competitors in a purely competitive market in which they have no control over the price they receive for produce or the prices they must pay for inputs. It is highly probable that they will continue to employ as many new methods as become known to them. They will try to earn some economic rent on the innovations; that is, an abnormal return to the enterprise relative to other farmers before other farmers adopt the technology. Thus, at any time there will probably still be considerable potential for more growth in productivity and production in the farm sector.

Continuing developments in mechanical and biological technology, the decline in the real price of capital relative to labor, and the emergence of a new agricultural managerial class will aggravate the "cost-price squeeze" in farming except for those operators who can increase scale and adopt technological improvement rapidly enough to offset the greater cash outlays required. This new capital-management era of farming will make it possible for supply response to be relatively elastic with regard to committing more capital resources and expanding output. The need to expand both acreage and enterprise size in order to realize economies of scale and to offset the higher overhead costs for modern capital inputs will produce a continued rise in the price of farm real estate. This rise in land prices will make it difficult for new farmers and those with limited capital to operate at a scale that will support a standard of living comparable to that provided by equivalent work in nonfarm occupations. Increased competition and commercialization of farming will again accelerate the exodus of labor from agriculture.

This type of adjustment to price changes in agriculture tends to keep supplies large and readily expansible while providing small or nonexistent profit margins for small operations. As will be shown in Chapter 2, such conditions give rise to income problems too broad to be readily solved by commodity programs in the form of subsidies. Although direct or indirect subsidies may increase the income of small producers, they provide even greater gain and incentive for larger producers already oriented to scale expansion and rapid incorporation of new technology. While some subsidies, if structured in a manner which does not increase supply and depress price, can make it possible for older operators to continue in subsistence operations until retirement, they offer little hope to young or beginning farmers who seek income and living standards comparable to that of workers at similar skill levels in nonfarm employment. The subsidies do not narrow the income gap between the typical small scale farms and the highly commercialized operations. They provide no compensation for that part of the farm labor force which finds itself replaced by modern technology. Those subsidies, both direct and indirect, which relate to units of input, output, or product transportation will always benefit large scale producers most. Since the large scale producer typically is more price responsive than the traditional small scale farmer, the per unit subsidies have a greater relative effect in increasing output of the former. Hence, with the greater output and lower prices inspired by the subsidy, the gain to the large commercial operator is expected to be proportionately greater than for the traditional small scale general operator.

The problems of adjustment have not been solved by the policies of the postwar decades, and more significantly, will not be solved in the future by a continuation of the same policies.

Distribution Problem. We indicated that the adjustment problem of the agricultural sector was caused partly by the strategies of individuals in adopting new technologies in the production process. The variation in individual farmers' abilities to adopt the technologies at sufficiently high levels to counteract the income-depressing influence of declining real returns leads to the change in income distribution within the farm sector. This is the essence of the distribution problem.

Another distribution problem can be, and has been, identified: that is the change in the share of national income accruing to the farm sector as economic development proceeds. Usually the farm sector in a developed nation shows a lower per capita income (for which GNP is a proxy) than the nonfarm sector. This has been true of Canada in the postwar years, as shown in Table 1.5. According to the projections contained in the table, the claim will likely remain true in the future. The table forecasts that, with the present set of policies in effect and the current rates of out-migration from agriculture maintained, the farm population on the average will still only earn half as great a per capita income as the nonfarm population in 1980.

This has led spokesmen for the agricultural sector to request policy instruments whose goals were to close the intersectoral income gap. In a sense, the interest groups have persuaded policy makers to view the national economy as having two sectors, a leading sector and a lagging sector (the agricultural sector), and as in the case of dualistic economies, developed or undeveloped, to seek to close the gap by raising the average income level of farmers. The average could be raised by (1) reducing the number of farmers while keeping the total sector income stable, (2) raising the incomes of the wealthiest farmers by an amount proportionally greater than their numbers, (3) raising

Table 1.5. Agriculture in the Economy, Selected Years 1930-67, and Projections to 1980

	1930	1940	1950	1960	1967	1980[a]
Total population (million)	10.4	11.5	14.0	18.2	20.0	26.0
Farm population as percentage of total[b]	31.7	27.4	20.8	11.7	9.8	6.0
Agriculture's addition to GNP ($ million)[c]	628	693	1,716	1,745	2,479	4,792
Percentage of GNP	10.9	10.3	9.5	4.8	4.6	3.0
Per capita GNP in agriculture as percentage of average per capita GNP[d]	0.34	0.38	0.46	0.41	0.47	0.50

Source: G. R. Purnell and V. A. Heighton, The Agricultural Situation in Canada, in Can. Farm Econ., Canadian Dept. of Agr., December 1970, pp. 1-15.
[a]Projections, except for population, are based on compound growth rates from 1962 to 1967. Population living on farms is projected on 1961-66 rate of change. Rural population in 1980 is an estimate of the Economic Council of Canada, Fifth Annual Review, Sept. 1968.
[b]Population figures are for census years 1931, 1941, 1951, 1961, and 1966.
[c]Values in current dollars.
[d]Calculated as ratio of agriculture's percentage of GNP to farm population as percentage of total population.

every farmer's income by the same absolute amount, or (4) raising the incomes of the poorest farmers directly. Canadian agriculturists and policy makers have tended to favor means (1), (2), and (3), and generally ignore (4).

Among the often stated goals for the farm sector are stability of gross net farm income, increased outmigration from the sector, growing average net income per capita in agriculture, and the assurance of a minimum level of living for all rural people.[21] None of the policies employed to reach these goals actually

21. See, for example, McCalla, Appraisal of Agricultural Policies in Canada; or Federal Task Force on Agriculture, Canadian Agriculture in the Seventies, (Ottawa: Queen's Printer, 1970), Chap. 3. Both writers list these as the usual goals of Canadian agriculture in the recent and relevant past.

closed the gap between the rich and the poor in the rural community; that is, none of the policies closed the intrasectoral income gap. This becomes very evident when 1966 data for the Canadian agricultural sector are analyzed. For example, the 1966 Census of Agriculture shows that 55 percent of all farms had gross sales incomes of less than $5,000, and 22 percent had gross sales in excess of $10,000. Over 50 percent of all sales income going to agriculture went to the 18 percent of all farms whose individual gross incomes were over $15,000 each.[22]

In fact, as we will subsequently demonstrate, the present Canadian policy instruments for agriculture are economically impotent to close intrasectoral income gaps (one policy type tends to widen the gap), in addition to which they are only moderately successful in closing the income gap between farm and nonfarm sectors.[23] Apparently agricultural policy makers have failed on all counts because they have been satisfied with the limited objective of attempting to close intersectoral income gaps, an approach which is satisfied with dealing with impersonal commodity groupings and more or less ignoring the persistent and growing intrasector gap between those with high and those with low levels of economic well-being.

Canada's geographic diversity had led to a variation in the regional distribution of agricultural land and climatic endowments. Canadian agricultural output has a regional orientation by commodity: grain and cattle raising in the west; mixed farming, dairy, cattle feeding, and swine production in central Canada; and mixed farming on a smaller scale in the Maritimes.

22. For an analysis of the 1966 census, and the outlook for farm income, see W. L. Porteous, Canadian Farm Incomes and Distribution, paper presented to the Canadian Agricultural Outlook Conference, Ottawa, November 1969; G. R. Purnell and J. A. Heighton, The Agricultural Situation in Canada, Can. Farm Econ., Canadian Dept. of Agr., Ottawa, December 1970, pp. 1-15 (especially table 8, which shows the growth of this disparity over time and predicts an even greater disparity in 1980).

23. McCalla, Appraisal of Agricultural Policies in Canada, p. 18, reports other evidence and opinion that agricultural policy has cured neither the intersectoral nor intrasectoral income distribution disparities.

Because of the variance in the net-revenue-producing power of these different crops (a result of different demand elasticities and market conditions) a regional diversity of farm incomes has emerged. The situation has generally favored the producers of central and western regions, while maritime farmers have generally been poor.

It has long been said in Canada that "wheat is king," because it has been a prime agricultural earner in export markets, and accounts for about 40 percent of Canadian agricultural income. Consequently, Canadian agricultural policy has tended to deal with the problems of wheat and grains first, while adding other policy instruments as they were needed to counter the side effects of grain policy. This has created a policy structure in which grain is at the center and the others were attached in a lean-to fashion about it. Concentration of agricultural policy on the problems of certain commodities has therefore tended to favor the farm population in certain regions at the probable expense of those in other regions. By concentrating on commodities, and not the welfare of farm families directly, policy has tended to miss the income problems of entire regions. Policy has not helped in closing interregional income differences, and has probably created wider gaps.

While there are two major side definitions of the distribution problem, the farm-nonfarm divergence and the interregional divergence, the divergence of incomes between the rich and poor in the farm community as a whole bears closest consideration. If policy were directed at the needs of the relatively disadvantaged in agriculture without regard for region or commodity of major production, the problems of the distribution of income between regions and between producers of various commodities would be considerably, if not entirely, resolved. By concentrating on intrasectoral income distribution, policy makers could simultaneously be working toward closing the farm-nonfarm income gap. However, by concentrating on regions and commodities, policy makers in the past have missed the opportunity to create truly equitable programs that actually have the potential to realize the goals so strongly avowed.

2 Economic Failure of Canadian Agricultural Policy

IN THE PRECEDING CHAPTER evidence was presented which illustrates that the policies of the postwar period had failed to solve the fundamental problems of the agricultural sector: namely, the adjustment problem and the intrasectoral income distribution problem. The evidence for the claim that adjustment had not proceeded well was the presence of a persistent divergence between the average farm and nonfarm per capita income levels. In effect, we implicitly assumed that if adjustment had proceeded properly in the agricultural sector, incomes per capita would tend to be equal to those in the rest of the economy, or approximate these levels in a close range. We observed, however, that in the past and even within the foreseeable future the average nonfarm income would exceed that of the farm sector. The evidence shows, in effect, that the farm sector was operating in a suboptimal position relative to the nonfarm sector in terms of resource allocation, and adjustment was not effected. Other opinion was referred to in the preceding chapter which was consistent with the evidence and with our evaluation of that evidence.

In examining the internal workings of the policy instruments typically employed in Canadian agriculture, we shall construct economic models depicting them as they act. This will enable us to determine whether the mechanisms themselves actually generate a decline in the farm-nonfarm income gap and whether incomes become more evenly distributed in the farm sector under the programs. In fact we will be able to observe whether an individual farmer is made worse or better off by the implementation of the policy.

The degree to which a policy instrument closes the interregional income gap will not be discussed specifically, because if a program is not capable of solving the other two problems but distributes agricultural income more evenly across regions, it would still be a poor program. In this case the policy would have the effect of distributing more widely a bad and probably deteriorating agricultural situation. If a government had the resources to solve the interregional income distribution problem, it could do so in a way which solved the other two problems as well. Thus, we concentrate on a two-criterion judging standard.

Obviously not all programs are instituted with the avowed intention of making adjustment easier and distributing income more equitably. Yet it is these two goals that are claimed as the eventual targets of action, as has been explicitly stated in some of the literature referred to in the preceding chapter, and implicitly when the shorter-term objectives of organizations are followed to their logical conclusions. Hence, our criterion for judgment is at least consistent with the targets in the Canadian setting.

Another point should be mentioned at the outset: it involves the degree to which individual policy instruments are essentially unique in their operation. Many fewer real differences exist between programs than their titles would seem to imply. In a functional economic sense, a provincial producers' marketing board for beans and a board for tobacco can be considered as identical if both employ quotas, operate on behalf of the growers within a province, and attempt to get higher effective prices by restricting the supply which flows to market. Similarly if one provincial government pays part of the cost of land-clearing operations, and another pays part of the cost of lime or fertilizer for its producers, both are similar in the economic sense that they are subsidizing inputs into production. Extension services and fertilizer subsidies would be economically similar, because both are subsidies to production inputs—one for management, the other for purchased inputs. It is possible therefore to classify the various programs that have been instituted for various specific reasons by the nature of the economic linkages in the system involved.

With this in mind we suggest that three classes of policy mechanisms have been used in Canada: a subsidy per unit of input, an output price support or subsidy per unit of output, and supply control on the part of marketing boards. Supply control in Canada has typically revolved around a marketing board's assignment of delivery quotas to producers within its legal jurisdiction while leaving farmers free to make their own decisions as to the types and quantities of inputs they would employ. More recently Canadian officials have begun to restrict the amount of land going into production (e.g., the LIFT Program referred to in Chap. 1). This type of program for supply control has been widely used (and abused) in the United States, with only moderate successes. (A survey of alternate land retirement schemes, their costs and benefits is given in Appendix B.) Functionally it operates in much the same way as a quota; an economic agent would probably restrict his use of inputs if he were faced with a fixed market for output and given prices of inputs and outputs.

The large list of programs (Table 1.1) for which both provincial and federal governments appropriate and administer funds serves as a base for further classification of programs. Provincial producer marketing boards do not generally draw funds from the governments (except, perhaps, as grants for operations classified as "general" or "other" in the table) and so are not listed.

Distinguishing the programs whose effect is to subsidize inputs into production from those which offer a de facto support to the per unit price of output is relatively easy in most cases. For example, government expenditures on extension, research support, education assistance, and general administration (categories 4, 5, 6, and 7 in Table 1.1) can be considered government's assistance to the production input "technological advance." Part of the expenditure is for the generation of new techniques, breeds, and seeds; part is for the facilities in which such developments occur and are disseminated to students; part is for the more general dissemination of the technologies to the farm community as a whole; and part is for the support of the administrative structure guiding the process. There is also a strong element of support for the management input in the expenditures for extension services.

Further expenditures to subsidize the cost of production inputs are those for production assistance (category 1 in Table 1.1) in crops, land and water development, farm credit, and other production assistance. Production assistance for livestock would, on the other hand, be classified as support for the prices of livestock, since in the table this category includes the quality premium expenditures of provincial and federal governments for hogs, cheese, and lambs. Marketing assistance (category 2 in Table 1.1) would be in general a subsidy on input costs to the extent that farmers bear the costs of marketing their produce. On the other hand, when marketing assistance is interpreted as promotional activity, the expenditure can be considered as a price support. A list of the input subsidy measures as distinguished here is given in Table 2.1.

Programs of price support and income assistance (category 3 in Table 1.1) can generally be considered as subsidizing the product per unit price. Stabilization of prices would be a de facto subsidy because farmers would assign a higher probability to their price expectations under stability, and so their average expectation would be higher than if a stability program were not in effect. Emergency assistance and crop insurance would have the same effects.

There is some difficulty, however, in classifying the Feed Freight Assistance Program and the Temporary Wheat Reserves Storage Program. Both have elements of production input subsidy, the Feed Freight Program attempting to lower the price of feed for livestock producers in eastern Canada and British Columbia, and the storage program supporting the cost of maintaining stocks for prairie farmers. Both also have elements of product price support, the Feed Freight Program sup-

Table 2.1. Classification of Canadian Government Agricultural Programs by Operational Type

Programs to Subsidize Cost of Inputs	Programs to Subsidize Value of Output
Production assistance	Production assistance
Crops	Livestock
Land and water	
Labor services	Marketing assistance
Other	General
Credit	
	Price support
Marketing assistance	Stabilization
Grains	Dairy commission
Livestock	Dairy products subsidy
Fruit and vegetable	Crop insurance
Other	Wheat reserves storage
	Emergency weather assistance
Extension services	Other
Research	
Education	
Administration	
Feed freight assistance	
Value of expenditures (1966-67) ($ million) 254	Value of expenditures (1966-67) ($ million) 187

Note: Provincial producer marketing boards are not included.

porting the price of feed grown in the Prairie Provinces by assuring a demand, and the storage subsidy acting to stabilize prices and raise the expected price of grain.

While a prolonged debate over the appropriate classification of the various programs would be relatively unimportant for the purposes of this book, its significance is in showing that Canadian agricultural policy instruments are amenable to such a twofold division (threefold when producer marketing boards are included). As is demonstrated in Table 2.1, the annual commitment of government funds to both kinds of program is high, and reasonably equal in importance. We proceed, therefore, with the construction of three basic economic models for the analysis of the policy instruments. A discussion of the economics of producer marketing board operations is given first, followed by an examination of an input subsidy's operation and that of a product price support.

PRODUCER MARKETING BOARDS AND SUPPLY CONTROL

Approximately 120 provincially empowered compulsory producer marketing boards are in existence in Canada. The circumstances leading up to their creation in general originated in the 1930s when it was observed that the capacity of the nonfarm market to absorb all the potential output of the agricultural sector was limited. Foreign markets also had limited value in assuring a stable and growing demand for farm products. Similar conditions have persisted in Canada since that time, with no real expectation that they will ever change. Because they require legal sanction we can consider the existence of marketing boards to be a policy of government.

The supply of output from agriculture has the potential to grow with tremendous speed under the slightest positive economic encouragement. A large degree of excess capacity in committed and fixed resources in the sector accounts for this. If only a small percentage of the farmers increased their offerings, prices would fall as would the total revenue of the agricultural sector, because of the generally inelastic nature of consumer demand for basic foodstuffs. This has motivated the formation of boards for the control and management of output, to insure that it does not grow too rapidly relative to the growth in population and per capita income, these being the only effective demand shifters in the agricultural products market.[1] If the demand for commodities is elastic with respect to price, increases in output lead to increases in the sector's total revenue; hence for those products faced with such a demand, the need for producer marketing boards to manage output with an income motive diminishes.

While producer boards could attempt to alter the demand situation for their product (and in fact several boards do conduct promotional activities), these

1. Other treatments of Canadian supply management and control include G. A. Hiscocks, Supply Management: Definition, Techniques and Implications, Can. Farm Econ., Can. Dept. of Agr., Ottawa, June 1970; and Federal Task Force on Agriculture, Canadian Agriculture in the Seventies. (Ottawa: Queen's Printer, December 1969), Chap. 12.

attempts may not be able to shift demand for the commodity to a point necessary for the producers to expand output up to the limits of their resources. In any event, with the demand for all foods being more or less fixed for a given population and income, the gains of the promotional activity for one producer board would accrue at the expense of the producers of substitute commodities. Hence, if all boards of closely related products engaged in promotional activity, the funds spent by all would be largely wasted.

Realizing this, boards have concentrated on various means of control on the supply and production side including the restriction of inputs, and by defining a permissible maximum each individual may market. The method of directly regulating the level of production by quotas has not been instituted.

Marketing boards, as independent institutions, have frequently expanded their activities beyond those of promotion and supply management into the areas of organizing for collective selling of members' produce, and product market organization. Several boards conduct activities—such as selling the produce of their members in different markets that are not linked by effective arbitrage—in order to gain higher average prices. The board distributes the total proceeds among the member producers by paying a "pooled" or average price per unit. The practice in effect gives the member producer a per unit price in excess of the price which would be established in his local market, and so gives a de facto subsidy per unit of output. But the outcomes of this phenomenon will be discussed in the following section. Similarly, the boards' arranging of contracts between their members and potential buyers has the same effect as a subsidy paid per unit of output and will also be discussed below.

<u>A Model to Evaluate the Adjustment Aspects of the Policy</u>. Consider a comparative static model of a simple agriculture with an index of inputs, X, and an index of outputs, Y, facing an inelastic aggregate consumer demand in the time period involved. For simplicity, let prices of inputs be given and unaltered over the period under consideration. Assume numerical parame-

ters which are realistic approximations of the Canadian situation.

At the beginning of the period a representative sectoral production function[2] could be

$$Q_y = aX^{0.8} \qquad (2.1)$$

and an inelastic demand function could be

$$Q = bP^{-0.4} \qquad (2.2)$$

From Equation 2.1, an input-use equation can be derived

$$X = a^{-1.25}Q^{1.25} \qquad (2.3)$$

and, assuming profit maximization as a goal, a normative supply function would be[3]

$$Q_s = (0.8)^4 a^5 P_x^{-4} P_y^4 \qquad (2.4)$$

The initial market equilibrium would occur when supply equals demand. Thus the equilibrium quantities presented in Table 2.2 as the original solution are calculated directly from the preceding equations.

As is usual in the agricultural sector, persistent national economic development means technological changes and changing relative factor prices which exert continued upward pressure on the quantities supplied. (Technological change implies here both a change in knowledge and method, and a change in factor use under changed relative real prices of inputs. The factor mix changes are subsumed however.) This phenomenon was described in Chapter 1. These are the main shifters of the supply function. Simultaneously, demand shifts upward if only because of population growth, since at high levels of income, the income elasticity of demand is positive but very small. How-

2. A Cobb-Douglas (unrestricted) form is selected for ease in manipulation.

3. For derivation of the supply function from the production function see, for example, Earl O. Heady and John Dillon, Agricultural Production Functions (Ames: Iowa State Univ. Press, 1961), pp. 61-62.

Table 2.2. Market Solution of Farm Sector under Technological Change and Supply Management

Item	Original Solution	Solution with Technological Change and Demand Growth	Solution with Supply Management Scheme (with target price)
Market price, P_y	$P_1 = (0.8)^{-10/11} a^{-50/44} b^{10/44} P_x^{10/11}$	$P_2 = 0.83P_1$	$P_3 = 0.92P_1$
Market quantity, Q	$Q_1 = (0.8)^{4/11} a^{5/11} b^{10/11} P_x^{-4/11}$	$Q_2 = 1.18Q_1$	$Q_3 = 1.14Q_1$
Inputs used, X	$X_1 = (0.8)^{5/11} a^{-30/44} b^{50/44} P_x^{-5/11}$	$X_2 = 0.98X_1$*	$X_3 = 0.94X_1$
Total farm revenue, $TR = P_y \cdot Q$	$TR_1 = (0.8)^{-6/11} a^{-30/44} b^{50/44} P_x^{6/11}$	$TR_2 = 0.98TR_1$	$TR_3 = 1.05TR_1$
Total farm costs, $TC = X \cdot P_x$	$TC_1 = (0.8)^{5/11} a^{-30/44} b^{50/44} P_x^{6/11}$	$TC_2 = 0.98TC_1$	$TC_3 = 0.94TC_1$
Net farm revenue, $NR = TR - TC$	$NR_1 = (0.2)(0.8)^{-6/11} a^{-30/44} b^{50/44} P_x^{6/11}$	$NR_2 = 0.98NR_1$	$NR_3 = 1.50NR_1$

*Lower input use is consistent with greater output since technological change has made inputs more productive.

ever, demand generally remains inelastic with respect to price.

With these forces operative over a period of time, and with no supply control policy in effect, a new production function would be generated, Equation 2.5, as would a new demand function, Equation 2.6.

$$Q = 1.2aX^{0.8} \tag{2.5}$$

(considering no change in the elasticity of production).

$$Q = 1.1bP^{-0.4} \tag{2.6}$$

A new market equilibrium would occur with new prices, quantities, revenues, and·costs (subscript 2) in effect. These bear relationships to the initial equilibrium magnitudes (subscript 1) as given in Table 2.2. As a result of the changes in technology and population, both of which are characteristic of progress in a modern economy, the farm sector has lost both total revenue, as expected, and net revenue, probably because of the lag in resource adjustment and the fixing of committed inputs. Whatever disparity existed between farm and nonfarm sector incomes has worsened, assuming that real GNP has risen or remained constant. (A decline in GNP would generally be inconsistent with the outward shift in demand, but might lead to a rise in the absolute value of the price elasticity.)

Certainly farmers employing new technologies would have been vaguely aware that such a possibility could exist for the farm sector as a whole. Yet as individuals they would employ the new technology if it appeared profitable for their own farms. At the same time, since most new technology is bound up in new investment goods[4] many farmers would be excluded from

4. This is the embodiment hypothesis of technical progress; for further discussion see D. W. Jorgenson, The Embodiment Hypothesis, J. Political Economy, Feb. 1966, pp. 1-17; D. W. Jorgenson and Zvi Griliches, The Explanation of Productivity Change, Rev. Econ. Studies, July 1967, pp. 249-84; and Murray Brown, On the Theory and Measurement of Technological Change (Cambridge: Cambridge Univ. Press, 1966), especially Chap. 6.

adopting new methods because they could not afford the equipment. This would be the case with a farmer having too little collateral for credit, or current resources which could not generate an income sufficient to pay for new equipment. In short, he would be constrained from exploiting the benefits of a new production function.

It follows, therefore, that if the sector has become worse off in general, but the wealthiest farmers have improved their private terms of trade (or at least remained in equal terms) with the nonfarm sector, then the poorer farmers have lost proportionally more than the sector as a whole. The income disparity within the farm sector would have widened as a result of technical progress. (This point is picked up again below.)

Now, assume that farmers as a whole become dissatisfied with a free market operation and are successful in establishing a compulsory producer marketing board to control the output marketed. They embark on a commodity withholding action so that marketed quantities do not grow as much as technology would allow under free conditions. Suppose that instead of prices falling to 83 percent of their initial level, farmers under the guidance of their board withhold enough produce to meet a target of, let us say, an 8 percent decline in price. With negative supply management (activities aimed at reducing total supply and rationing the right to sell among producers), a new market equilibrium would result. This is given in Table 2.2 in terms of the original solution.

With the withholding action in effect, the net farm incomes of the sector would rise under the dual impetus of rising total revenue and declining production costs. Farmers would benefit from their own use of advanced technology. What is more, consumers would also be beneficiaries of the technological changes since they now could secure the same, or more, output at a lower price than in the original solution. Consumers would lose to the extent that the decreased use of inputs centered on purchased inputs. However, even if all the inputs foregone were purchases, this would only be a 6 percent reduction compared to the 8 percent gain brought about by the decline in farm prices. The supply control measure would tend to yield, in effect, a solution in which everyone would be at least as well-off as before the change occurred.

By setting a target level of input use rather than a target price level, the board could have gained the same result. But this would be true only if the reduction of inputs was sufficient to counteract the growth in productivity of inputs remaining in use.

Part of the reason for the failure of land-withholding programs in the United States has been that farmers have not been restrained from improving the productivity of the acreage farmed. They have tended to use the capital inputs normally assigned to the acres withdrawn on the acreage remaining in production. As a result those acres farmed have become even more productive than before the land retirement program, although at a diminishing rate. The same pattern of events could conceivably occur when any input is arbitrarily licensed. (A discussion of land retirement programs in alternate forms is given in Appendix B.)

The analysis so far indicates very little or nothing about the in-farm sector distribution aspects of the supply-withholding action. Neither does it indicate what would occur if some producers did not cooperate with the withholding action, if closely competitive products existed, or if political strength rested in the nonfarm sector.

Although it is theoretically possible for producers as a whole to increase net farm income by withholding produce from the market, they will only be successful in maintaining their gains if the board and the product display certain characteristics. It is generally recognized that a market withholding action will only succeed in bringing about an improvement in price and total net revenue when all producers of the particular commodity selling in the same market participate in the action. If there are "nonboard" producers selling in essentially the same market as the group restricting their output, the efforts of the board producers will be partially, if not totally, frustrated.

What constitutes "essentially the same market" is of course a function of several factors which include the degree of substitutability between the commodities, the state of transportation facilities, the advance of transportation technology, the state of food processing, and the state of communications. For example, one would expect the typical market for fluid milk to expand and become more homogeneous as the ease, speed, and preserving technologies associated with the transportation industry advance; to progress further as filled or artificial milks develop; and to advance even further in these directions as communications in conjunction with transport make arbitrage more feasible over expanded areas. With the further advance in the technologies of agricultural-related industries, the possibilities of having both board and nonboard agents acting in the same market increase.

The significance of universal participation (and by implication, nonuniversal participation) can be illustrated with a simple numerical example. Consider a market demand schedule, inelastic with respect to price,

$$Q_D = 15 - P_y \qquad (2.7)$$

and a market supply schedule, Equation 2.8, which is the sum of a marketing board's offering, Equation 2.9, and a nonboard offering, Equation 2.10:

$$Q_S = 2P_y + 2P_x^{-1} + 1 \qquad (2.8)$$

$$Q_B = P_y + P_x^{-1} + 1 \qquad (2.9)$$

$$Q_N = P_y + P_x^{-1} \qquad (2.10)$$

P_x is the price index of factors of production, and P_y is the price of the commodity. Clearly the board offer is larger than the nonboard offer. When the price of inputs is 1, a market equilibrium occurs when supply equals demand. The resulting equilibrium magnitudes are given in Table 2.3.

If the board undertakes to reduce its output under a scheme of producer quotas or by other means by, for

Table 2.3. Market Solution for Board and Nonboard Farmers under Supply Management

Item	Original Solution (units)	Solution with Supply Management (units)
Market price	4	4.5
Market sales	11	10.5
Board	6	5.0 (target)
Nonboard	5	5.5
Total revenue	44	47.25
Board	24	22.5
Nonboard	20	24.75
Net revenue[a]		
Board	23	21.67
Nonboard	19	23.55

[a]Calculated assuming $P_x = 1$, initial input level = 1 unit, and elasticity of production = 1, for both board and nonboard members.

example, 17 percent (from 6 units to 5) with the hope of improving the price and income situation for its farmers, but the nonboard farmers do not, the supply function would shift backward to Equation 2.11. The demand function remains as Equation 2.7.

$$Q'_S = (P_y + 1) + 5 \tag{2.11}$$

Under these circumstances ($P_x = 1$), a new market equilibrium would result with magnitudes given in Table 2.3. Although there has been a 12.5 percent higher market price and only 4.6 percent decline in sales (resulting in a 7.4 percent increase in total sectoral revenues), board members have experienced a 6 percent decline in their total revenues. On the other hand, nonboard members have experienced increased total revenues of about 23.5 percent. Nonboard members have, in effect, gained as freeloaders at the expense of the board-regulated farmers.

Even if we consider that board members would reduce their total expenses while nonboard members add to their total costs, the outcome would be practically the same. If both producer groups have similar production characteristics with, for example, Ep (production elasticity) = 1, the 17 percent decline in output offered by board members would lead to their using 17 percent fewer inputs while nonboard producers would use 20 percent more. Under initial input price conditions, P_x = 1, and assuming 1 unit of input initially used, initial net revenues would be 23 for board members, and 19 for nonboard members. After the market withholding, board member net revenue would be 21.67 (a loss of 5.8 percent) while nonboard net revenue is 23.55 (a 24 percent increase over 19).

With this demonstrable inequality in the distribution of the benefits of the board's actions, it is clear why board organizers have sought to make membership in the boards compulsory for all producers of a similar commodity. The market has been generally subdivided among the members under quota systems (primarily delivery quotas), with quota being distributed among producers in relation to a given criterion.[5] The criteria in the initial allocation of quota would probably reflect the preboard distribution of market shares in order to insure compliance of the largest producers, but this is not the only means.

The ease or difficulty of insulating a market from the commodities produced by nonboard members depends on the factors which we previously considered in indicating the conditions under which producers can be viewed as being in the same economic market. In this case, the worse the state of transportation, communications, and food preservation technologies, and the fewer the substitutes, the higher the degree to which a market can be isolated.

Historically in Canada population centers have been geographically spread out sufficiently that provincial

---

5. There have been considerable discussion about, and attempts to overcome, the effects of quotas on economic efficiency, on freezing a production process into set patterns, on the frustration of technological advances and resource mobility, and on capitalization of benefits into land prices. Even though a marketing board could potentially diminish the disparity between farm and nonfarm incomes, such a mechanism offers no hope of diminishing the disparity in incomes within the agricultural sector. Quota systems are discussed in a report by the Federal Task Force, Canadian Agriculture in the Seventies, Chap. 12.

boundaries have served reasonably well as the bounds of jurisdiction for marketing boards. Gradual technological advances in the transportation industry have tended to create the situation in which producers in contiguous provinces, offering the same commodity in their respective markets, could begin to suffer, or gain, because advances in transportation technology have tended to bring producers together into more common markets in spite of geography. For example, the producers of hogs in one province might withhold produce to improve the provincial price level while the producers in the neighboring province have no board. But being unable to legislate which market buyers patronize, producers in the restricting province lose sales as buyers go to the markets in the unrestricting province (at least to markets that are feasible under the state of transportation technology). It will be recalled that early attempts to form boards in Canada were ruled unconstitutional because they attempted to interfere with interprovincial trade.

In spite of this, there has been, over the past few decades, little enthusiasm for national marketing boards with regulatory powers. Provincial boards seem to have been content with minor losses due to improved flexibility in transport and other related technologies, rather than risk the consequences of national action which could reduce the output of various crops in certain provinces.

As recently as March 1970, there has been a federal government initiative to introduce legislation to permit the formation of national marketing boards. The proposed powers of the board, except those of designing, reviewing, and supervising the operation of marketing plans and agencies under the act,[6] were undefined at the time of writing. The change in direction is significant, however, and seems to recognize the logic of the model given above.

The model depicting a policy of permitting marketing boards to function as instruments for supply con-

---

6. A brief description is given in Hiscocks, Supply Management, p. 4.

trol attempted to determine whether the policy created or prolonged the life of Canada's farm-nonfarm income gap problem. The analysis reported in Table 2.2 shows that supply control would and could close the intersectoral income gap. Thus we conclude that supply control alone is not responsible for the continued existence of the adjustment problem.

However, we have not ruled out the possibility that the typical application of quota systems could nullify the possible gains to the agricultural sector that supply control could yield. Quite clearly, quota systems can retard mobility within agriculture. (See footnote 5.) Yet what is significant is that one can favor the principle of supply control as a means of attaining a Pareto Optimal outcome of the changes brought about by progress for farm and nonfarm communities, without having to rely on arbitrary quotas as part of the system. We will demonstrate in Chapter 8 various alternative instruments which could be put into operation by the existing set of provincial marketing boards that would avoid the quota problem but still yield positive results for agriculture.

<u>A Model to Evaluate the Income Distribution Aspects of the Policy</u>. To evaluate the impact of a government policy of negative supply control on the income distribution problem, two production functions are considered. The first, Equation 2.12, represents the aggregate farm production function for a set of typical large farms, while Equation 2.13 represents that of a set of typical small farms. We could assume that each production function represents only one farm, and that there are n large farms and m small farms (with an aggregation procedure employed to get the market supply function), but it is sufficient for the demonstration to assume that the two production functions given represent the class. The individual large farm could be represented by an n^{-1} share of the aggregate under a set of strict assumptions.

Production function 2.12 exhibits a lower elasticity of production, which is consistent with the producer's being further along in the economic range of production (closer to the upper end of the economic range of production,[7] and closer to the point where the marginal return to added inputs is zero). Such a set of producers would logically be in this position relative to smaller producers who do not employ the capital inputs that the larger producers employ, only because the smaller producers are constrained by lack of credit for expansion or an inadequate base upon which to build an expanded enterprise (e.g., poorer climate and land, labor and other shortages, etc.). In addition, if the poorer farmers were ignorant of the technology that the larger farmer employed (not just constrained from using it) the outcomes of the following analysis would be even less favorable to the smaller farmer. Thus we assume the most generous possible set of circumstances for the smaller farmer.

$$q_1 = 10 + 8X_1^{0.5} \tag{2.12}$$

$$q_2 = 5 + 5X_2^{0.5} \tag{2.13}$$

where q is the amount of physical output produced, and X is a set of inputs. The square root form of the production function is used only as an illustration, and is selected because of its property of yielding easily added supply functions.

From the production functions 2.12 and 2.13 are derived the normative farm-set supply functions 2.14 and 2.15 respectively:

$$Q_{s1} = 10 + 32P_y P_x^{-1} \tag{2.14}$$

$$Q_{s2} = 5 + 12.5P_y P_x^{-1} \tag{2.15}$$

Q_s is the output from the set of farms, P_y is the

7. We assume that in an ex ante sense there is one production function for an agricultural enterprise which incorporates all the latest technology. What one observes in the statistical description of production functions is the ex post outcome of farmers who are constrained in various ways from achieving the ex ante production function.

product price, and P_x is the input price. These are added to get the market supply function 2.16:

$$Q_m = 15 + 44.5P_y P_x^{-1} \tag{2.16}$$

Let a market demand be represented by Equation 2.17,

$$Q_D = 60 - 0.5P_y \tag{2.17}$$

(Q_D is the quantity demanded) which is inelastic with respect to product prices when

$$60 > P_y > 0$$

The established market price when supply equals demand in equilibrium will be of the form

$$P_{yE} = 45P_x(44.5 + 0.5P_x)^{-1}$$

To investigate the distribution problems most likely to occur for the farm sector we specify that the product price at equilibrium should fall within the inelastic range indicated above. Thus, there is a range of input prices which would be consistent with the inelastic product price range. Product prices will fall within the inelastic range if input prices fall in the range $178 > P_x > 0$. For ease in the following calculations we arbitrarily select $P_x = 111$ units. Thus P_y can be assigned the value 49.95 units (without intending the value to necessarily represent dollars).

For these magnitudes, a full market solution can be calculated. Such a solution is given in Table 2.4, in which the appropriate magnitudes for significant variables for the market as a whole and for each producer group are indicated.

If there is a change in technology (both increased productivity of inputs and changed input mix if any occurs) resulting from its general advancement, let us suppose it means a 20 percent improvement in the productivity of agricultural inputs as a package. We assume the least possible impact of this technical

Table 2.4. Market Solution for Farm Sector and Two Producer Groups and Different Elasticities of Production under Inelastic Commodity Demand

Item	Market	Producer 1 (larger scale)	Producer 2 (smaller scale)
Market price	49.95	49.95	49.95
Market quantity	35.00	24.4 (70%)	10.6 (30%)
Inputs used	4.49	3.24	1.25
Total farm revenue	1,748.25	1,218.78	529.48
Total farm costs	498.39	359.64	138.75
Net farm revenue	1,249.84	859.14	390.73
Share of total net revenue (%)	...	68.5	31.5

change on the agricultural sector by assuming that the elasticity of production is not changed. In addition, suppose that there is a growth in income and population such that there is a 10 percent growth in general demand, but not a change in the price elasticity of demand. In these circumstances the production functions of the large and small producers become

$$q_1 = 1.2(10 + 8X^{0.5}) \tag{2.18}$$

$$q_2 = 1.2(5 + 5X^{0.5}) \tag{2.19}$$

These in turn give the supply functions for the set of large and small producers and the aggregate respectively as

$$Q_{s1} = 12 + 34.56P_yP_x^{-1} \tag{2.20}$$

$$Q_{s2} = 6 + 18.00P_yP_x^{-1} \tag{2.21}$$

$$Q_m = 18 + 52.56P_yP_x^{-1} \tag{2.22}$$

The demand function becomes

$$Q_D = 66 - 0.55P_y \tag{2.23}$$

In market equilibrium, the product price is expressed in the form

$$P_y = 48P_x(52.56 + 0.55P_x)^{-1}$$

which, when the input price is again assumed to be $P_x = 111$, as above, takes the magnitude $P_y = 46.86$. The remaining magnitudes and the respective net income positions of the two producers are given in Table 2.5.

As a result of the technical change and the simultaneous growth in demand, the product price has fallen by 6 percent of the original and the quantity sold has increased in total by 15 percent. However, the total increase in marketed quantity resulted from a considerable expansion on the part of the smaller producers, who raised their share of total marketing from 30 percent to about 33 percent of the total. This would be expected because, with higher production elasticity, they would exhibit a higher price elasticity of supply. But their expansion in total output has meant that their inputs have increased proportionally more than those of the larger producer, and their net revenue position has worsened. This follows because there would still be scale economies in further expansion if financial constraints were not binding. They now have a smaller share of total net revenue than before the technical change. It is as if the larger farmers viewed the technical change and the growth in demand as an opportunity to economize on inputs (their input use declines by 30 percent), and the smaller farmers view the changes as an incentive to expand the scale of operations. Small farmers are not irrational in following this course of action, since they would still be expanding to the point when marginal cost equals marginal revenue. The difficulty is that their expansion has reduced market prices and increased their own costs.

If producers attempt supply control and management to retain some of the benefits of the technological and demand change, they could generally do so, as shown above. At the same time the nonfarm sector would have more produce at lower prices than originally. Suppose a marketing board sets a per unit price tar-

Table 2.5. Market Solution for Farm Sector and Two Producer Groups with 20 Percent Growth in Technology and 10 Percent Shift in Commodity Demand

Item	Market	Producer 1	Producer 2
Market price	46.86 (0.94P_1)	46.84	46.84
Market quantity	40.2 (1.15Q_1)	26.6 (1.09Q_1)(67%)	13.6 (1.28Q_1)(33%)
Inputs used	3.84	2.25	1.59
Total farm revenue	1,846.29	1,246.48	599.81
Total farm costs	426.24	249.75	176.49
Net farm revenue	1,420.05	996.73	423.32
Share of total net revenue (%)	...	70.2	29.8

get of $0.97P_y$; that is, it will permit a 3 percent fall in product price (but not the 6 percent that unrestrained marketings would produce). This would mean that the market would clear if 39.3 units of output were offered at 48.5 money units per unit. There would be a greater volume of output than in the original case, but 2 percent less output than in the unrestricted case.

The immediate problem for the board, however, would be to ration the 39.3 units among the producers. Board management would have three options in this regard:

1. Distribute quota in proportion to "historical" market shares, which means permitting the pretechnological change shares (70/30) to prevail;
2. Distribute quota in proportion to posttechnological market shares, as if the market were allowed to determine the solution freely (67/33); or
3. Distribute quota in a way biased toward the smaller producer (e.g., 65/35 or any other such ratio).

If the board is politically responsive, either internally or because of government supervision, option 1 is most likely to be adopted; option 2 would possibly be adopted; but option 3 would not likely be adopted.

The reasons for this ranking are straightforward. The universal participation of all producers of the commodity to be controlled in the withholding action is essential for the success of the operation, as has been shown above. To get this universal participation, guarantees would have to be given to large producers that no producer would be asked to sacrifice his relative position if a board were formed. In an established board, guarantees would be required to restrain large producers from breaking away from board control, possibly forming a black market. Thus historic shares would be most likely to occur. However, universal participation could still be insured and justly enforced through law if producers were at least guaranteed their relative position, assuming employment of new technology. The most the low income farmers could expect would be a growth in their share of the market appropriate to the gains they would otherwise earn in the posttechnological change economy. In the example, to guarantee low income producers more than the 33 percent share (their share if output were not controlled in the new technology area) would prompt the larger producers to leave the board and so benefit from the withholding action of the others, as in the mechanism shown above, or not give approval to the formation of the board in the first place. Therefore only option 1 or 2 would be acceptable. (A proposal that the government give it power to enforce compulsory membership was rejected by Ontario egg producers in 1968, in part because the board proposed to redistribute excess market shares of quota among the poorer, smaller farmers, and so increase the share going to small producers.)

The solution that would result under either of these options is given in Table 2.6. It is evident that the net income gap is not closed in either case. In fact, with historical shares obtaining, the in-sector income distribution is worsened. Thus, even though a restriction of the market offering can increase the total net revenue to the farm sector, it can do nothing to improve the distribution of income within the farm sector.

SUBSIDIES PER UNIT OF INPUT

Conceptually, any activity of government or other agency, which allows farmers to produce output at lower average costs than they would bear if they were farming as private individuals facing normal input price conditions in their area constitutes a de facto subsidy on inputs. This means that there is a measurable value to the subsidy. The value is the difference between the market value of the input and the price the farm sector pays for it. It may be difficult to identify the precise input being subsidized in some cases, but in general the identification is not obscure.

In Table 2.1, for example, a list of government programs was presented which are subsidies on purchased inputs under the definition just given. These include subsidies to assist in the purchase of lime in

Table 2.6. Market Solution for Farm Sector and Two Producer Groups under Different Quota Systems, during Output Withholding Action of 3 Percent

Item	Market		Traditional Shares		Posttechnical Change Shares	
			1 (70%)	2 (30%)	1 (67%)	2 (33%)
Market price	48.50		48.50	48.50	48.50	48.50
Market quantity	39.30		27.50	11.80	26.20	13.10
Inputs used[a]	(3.48)	(3.55)	2.56	0.92	2.16	1.39
Total farm revenue	1,905.75		1,333.75	572.00	1,270.70	635.05
Total farm costs[a]	(386.28)	(493.99)	284.16	102.12	239.70	154.29
Net farm revenue[a]	(1,419.47)	(1,512.76)	1,049.59	369.88	1,031.00	481.71
Share of total net revenue (%)	...		74	26	68	32

[a]Under two quota regimes.

the Prairie Provinces, the acquisition of low interest credit, and so on. Further, programs exist which clearly subsidize management to the extent that extension services, educational support, and research contribute to better farm practices. Of more importance have been the large investments that government has made in the development of advanced biological inputs and disease control as a general subsidy and stimulus to technological change. Mechanical inventions and innovations embodied in advanced equipment have generally been sold to farmers by machinery companies.

If transportation costs are viewed as costs of production, government programs have subsidized inputs further. The Feed Freight Assistance Program has, as argued elsewhere, at least served to establish a ceiling price for the trade in feed grains in eastern Canada and British Columbia and so has tended to hold down the price of purchased feed. By paying the costs of transporting grain from the Lakehead to points in eastern Canada, and from the Peace River Block to British Columbia, government has insured that a large volume of grain would be available at Lakehead and Peace River prices anywhere in eastern Canada or British Columbia. Thus there is pressure on grain prices in the two regions to approximate those at Lakehead and Peace River.[8] Marketing costs have also been partially subsidized, federally and provincially.

In operation, the subsidy on inputs has the effect of creating demand for the subsidized production input, a fact which has been used in some developing nations to encourage the use of fertilizers, new varieties of seed, and other nonfarm-originating inputs. In more advanced nations, the effect would more nearly be to increase existing demands directly for nonfarm inputs. This observation leads to an important conclusion on the latent potential of farm relief programs paid on the basis of the volume of inputs used to become de facto input subsidies, and the more general question of how an input price-support program should operate

8. See Acres Research and Planning, "Problems, Policies and Prospects for the Feedgrain-Livestock Economy," report to the Federal Task Force on Agriculture, 1969, vol. 4, pp. 89-101. Available at the Canadian Dept. of Agr. Library, Ottawa.

to insure that net income will increase for farm families. The problem revolves around the frequency and certainty of such assistance.

If input-related assistance takes the form of rebates (once-only payments after production decisions have been made) then they would certainly improve the one-period, net income position of recipients, and the payment will be like a windfall gain. However, if the assistance becomes institutionalized, as it has in the case of farm credit, prairie lime, and so on, farm managers will use the effectively lower price in their planning calculations, and the aim of the subsidy, to improve net incomes, will be frustrated in most cases after one or two production periods. Such will be the effects of subsidies both on material and management inputs.

We will show in the model below that the distortion in input market prices will lead to a situation in which the main beneficiaries of the subsidy will be in the nonfarm sector.

A Model to Evaluate the Adjustment Aspects of the Policy. The policy operation can be illustrated by modifying the model developed to consider the supply control policy. The model is applied to the sector as a whole and makes no initial distinction between subgroups within the sector. We assume that the production function, Equation 2.1, and the demand function, Equation 2.2, still apply. In this model, we examine the input-use behavior of farmers, so the demand function for inputs, Equation 2.24, is derived from Equation 2.1. The normative supply function is given in Equation 2.25:

$$X = [(0.8)aP_y P_x^{-1}]^5 \qquad (2.24)$$

$$Q_s = (0.8)^4 a^5 P_y^4 P_x^{-4} \qquad (2.25)$$

The market equilibrium magnitudes in this unrestricted case are those given in the "original solution" in Table 2.2. (See Table 2.7.)

Let us assume that a program is put into effect which constitutes a subsidy on inputs, and which lasts

Table 2.7. Market Solution with Input Price Subsidy of 10 Percent, and Elastic and Inelastic Commodity Demand

Item	Elasticity of Production of 0.8		Elasticity of Production of 0.5[a]	
	Inelastic commodity demand[b]	Elastic commodity demand[c]	Inelastic commodity demand	Elastic commodity demand
Market price, P_y	$P_2 = 0.91P_1$	$P_2 = 0.93P_1$	$P_2 = 0.93P_1$	$P_2 = 0.96P_1$
Market quantity, Q	$Q_2 = 1.04Q_1$	$Q_2 = 1.11Q_1$	$Q_2 = 1.03Q_1$	$Q_2 = 1.06Q_1$
Inputs used, X	$X_2 = 1.04X_1$	$X_2 = 1.14X_1$	$X_2 = 1.06X_1$	$X_2 = 1.13X_1$
Total farm revenue, $TR = Q \cdot P_y$	$TR_2 = 0.95TR_1$	$TR_2 = 1.04TR_1$	$TR_2 = 0.96TR_1$	$TR_2 = 1.02TR_1$
Total farm costs, $TC = X \cdot P_x$	$TC_2 = 0.94TC_1$	$TC_2 = 1.03TC_1$	$TC_2 = 0.95TC_1$	$TC_2 = 1.13TC_1$
Net farm revenue, $NR = TR - TC$	$NR_2 = 0.99NR_1$	$NR_2 = 1.07NR_1$	$NR_2 = 0.95NR_1$	$NR_2 = 1.02NR_1$

[a]Magnitudes subscripted 1 are found by replacing the production function in the "original solution" with one having a production elasticity of 0.5.
[b]Magnitudes of the variables subscripted 1 are given in Table 2.2 as "original solution." Original solution is that obtaining without an input price subsidy.
[c]Magnitudes subscripted 1 are found by using a price-elastic demand function in the "original solution" of Table 2.2.

for more than one production period, so that farmers can adjust their levels of inputs under profit maximization principles. If the input price is effectively reduced so that $P_{x2} = 0.9P_{x1}$, the aggregate demand for production inputs will shift. We assume for further convenience that increased demand for production inputs will not put upward pressure on market prices. If prices for inputs rise as a result of the shift in demand, the subsidy could still be made large enough to reduce the on-farm price of resources shown in the example. Other potential problems, such as input suppliers raising prices because they know a government subsidy will obtain, or imperfections in distribution, manufacture, and other sectors, are peripheral to the analysis at hand and will not be discussed. For this example, no embodied technical changes are allowed, so newly purchased inputs exhibit the same per unit productivity as the old. The new level of resource use (subscript 2) will be

$$X_2 = (0.8)^5 a^5 P_y^5 P_{x1}^{-5} (0.9)^{-5} \qquad (2.26)$$
$$= 1.635X_1$$

in terms of old production input prices. A new normative supply function will become

$$Q_{s2} = (1.635)^{0.8} (0.8)^4 a^5 P_y^4 P_x^{-4} \qquad (2.27)$$
$$= 1.472Q_{s1}$$

In the previous model in which the intent was to examine the problems of supply control, the supply schedule shifted under the forces of technological change resulting from general economic progress. Here, however, we are interested in isolating the influences of the input price subsidy, and we wish to shift the supply schedule only under input-use pressure. To preserve the consistency of the model, we assume that demand does not shift either.

The market equilibrium magnitudes are presented in Table 2.7, as expressed in terms of the original equilibrium magnitudes. The reduced cost of inputs has increased their use, and the net effect of the production response (damped, since the elasticity of production in Equation 2.1 is 0.8), the decline in market price of the commodity, and the reduced price of inputs has been to increase sales volume slightly. But the net revenue for the farm sector has declined, indicating that not only has the subsidy failed to close the farm-nonfarm income gap, but that the gap has tended to widen.

This is clear evidence that the payment of input price subsidies tends to retard adjustment. The model showed that if the acquisition price of a resource falls, but the expected profitability of the input rises, remains constant, or falls at a slower rate, the resource becomes more valuable; hence it is less likely to leave its current agricultural employment, be that on a specific farm or in the sector as a whole. This conclusion anticipates the result of the experiment to examine the intrasectoral distribution effects of the input price subsidy to be given below—that the input price subsidy cannot help close the intrasectoral income gap.

When consumer demand is elastic there is reason to suspect that the effects of the subsidy would differ considerably. In this case, an increase in output leads to a growth in total sectoral revenue, so that it is possible for farmers to gain from the input subsidy.

Using the same production function, Equation 2.1, same producer demand for resources, Equation 2.24, and normative supply functions as above, Equation 2.25, and an aggregate consumer demand function

$$Q_D = b.P^{-1.5} \qquad (2.28)$$

a market equilibrium will be established. Now, if a program subsidizes input costs which reduced the on-farm costs by 10 percent ($P_{x2} = 0.9P_{x1}$), a new equilibrium would occur. This is also given in Table 2.7. In the case where consumer demand for the commodity is elastic with respect to product price, the net revenue of the farm sector increases within the presence of input price subsidy. Farmers thus retain some of the benefits originally intended for them in the program. But clearly they do not retain the full value of the program as set out. The rise in net revenue under the program is only 7 percent, while the subsidy paid is 10 percent of the input price. This damped effect is due in part to the fact that the elasticity of production of the production function, Equation 2.1, is less than unity. Hence, with this production function, output would increase by a smaller percentage than the growth in inputs used. The relatively smaller growth in output would mean that total revenue would tend to grow more slowly than the increase in input use. With the growth in input use, total costs would rise with the effect that the input price subsidy would have a somewhat reduced impact on net revenue. If consumer demand displayed unitary elasticity with respect to product price, there would be no change in net revenue for the farm sector when a subsidy on input prices is paid. This can be demonstrated by reworking the model with demand schedule $Q = bP_Y^{-1.0}$. We would see that in the initial solution $NR_1 = (0.2)b$. In the solution with the subsidy in effect, $P_2 = 0.92P_1$, $Q_2 = 1.08Q_1$, $TR_2 = 0.995TR_1$, $TC_2 = 0.992TC_1$, and $NR_2 = 0.2b$.

The result demonstrates that the retained benefit of an input subsidy for the farm sector varies with the elasticity of demand for the product. It is reasonably accepted that as economic growth and development proceed, the price elasticity of demand declines. It is immediately suggested that as development occurs and progress is made, the subsidy on input prices as a means of farm support offers decreased benefits and eventually serves to penalize the sector.

It is also realized that as economic progress occurs there is a tendency for the agricultural sector to exhaust more of the efficiencies and scale economies known to it. (Implied here is the notion that no major technological breakthrough occurs in the two or three production cycles needed for this result to be realized.) Over time there is a tendency for the elasticity of production to decline as well as the price elasticity of demand.

But even as the elasticity of production varies, it is clear that the same tendency for the farm sector to gain less than the full benefit of the subsidy when demand is elastic and to lose net income when demand is inelastic will exist. This can be readily demonstrated by reestimating the original solutions and the solutions with a 10 percent input price subsidy using the production function

$$Q = aX^{0.5} \qquad (2.29)$$

in place of Equation 2.1. The market equilibrium solutions, when demand is inelastic as in Equation 2.2, and when it is elastic as in Equation 2.28, can easily be calculated. Table 2.7 shows that with inelastic demand the incidence of a 10 percent subsidy paid on the price of inputs reduces the net income of the sector, and the same subsidy paid when demand is elastic holds some (damped) benefits.

Comparison of the results that obtain in the different elasticities of production (Table 2.7) indicates that the farm sector is likely to lose any benefits from input subsidies very quickly as progress occurs. The comparison shows that when the sector has the possibility of gaining (in the elastic range of demand), it will gain proportionally less, given a demand situation, when the elasticity of production is less. When the sector would expect to suffer losses by having the subsidy in effect (in the inelastic range of demand), the sector loses proportionally more with a lower production elasticity. Thus, with economic progress, the potential gains from the existence of a subsidy on inputs will tend to be dissipated quickly, making the subsidy a liability.

Of course, the analysis just completed was made on the assumption that there would be no major technological innovations to effectively upset the marginal conditions implied in the calculations. But this assumption could be relaxed without nullifying the tendencies suggested by the preceding conclusions. For example, if technological innovation proceeds at a regular pace in regular and small increments, this would tend to put upward pressure on the elasticity of production and could continue to counteract the net income-depressing influences of declining elasticity of demand. For another example, a large and discrete technological breakthrough could raise the elasticity of production dramatically (a break, perhaps of the significance of the Green Revolution in Asia) so that government subsidies to encourage the use of the new inputs could yield benefits for farm and nonfarm sectors. But even this would occur only if demand were elastic. If demand were inelastic only the nonfarm sector would benefit from the government programs.

For Canada in the postwar decades, it is clear that the demand for agricultural products has been uniformly inelastic with respect to price. Thus, the continuance of the payment of input subsidies could only continue to tax the farm sector for the benefit of the nonfarm sector. The degree to which the tax is borne by various groups within the sector would depend on the elasticity of demand for the specific product, and whether or not the inputs into that product are subsidized. This latter condition was clearly present, however. We can conclude that the payment of input subsidies has not served the adjustment process well and can be considered one of the barriers to future adjustment if continued.

Does this mean that all subsidies on inputs for agriculture should be dropped? Probably not, since from the nation's point of view the agricultural sector is a provider of vital inputs into the rest of the economy. To the extent that the nation has growing use for agricultural output, it may be wise to continue subsidizing the sector and exploit it for the benefit of the rest of the economy. Certainly this attitude would not be new in Canada, as shown in the review of the history of policy. But the continued value of such subsidies is questionable as a policy measure for the benefit of the farm sector. Taking a broader view, the future national cost of retarded adjustment in agriculture may in fact be more than the further expected benefits from such programs. Some alternate possibilities are outlined in Part 2 which have lower national cost for the same national benefits, while insuring that the farm sector shares in the benefits.

A Model to Evaluate the Income Distribution Aspect of the Policy. The comparison between the cases in which net revenue declined under the influence of an input subsidy and inelastic consumer demand was made to show the differences in the effects of the subsidy as the elasticity of production changed over time. No effort was made to insure that the equilibrium price would be the same in both situations, and the example cannot be used to imply a solution to the distribution problem between sets of large and small farmers. Yet the preceding analysis did suggest that the revaluation of production inputs under the payment of input subsidies and the retardation of the adjustment processes resulting from this appreciation would probably not assist the distribution of income in the sector.

The model to examine the intrasectoral income distribution impact of supply management presented earlier is now modified to examine the distributional aspects of the input subsidy. The production functions for the set of large and small farmers, Equations 2.12 and 2.13, are retained as is the market demand function, Equation 2.17. The derived normative supply functions for inputs are Equations 2.30 and 2.31:

$$X_1 = 16.P_y^2 P_x^{-2} \tag{2.30}$$

$$X_2 = 6.25P_y^2 P_x^{-2} \tag{2.31}$$

The original market solution, under the assumption that input price can be represented by the magnitude $P_x = 111$, is that given in Table 2.4. (See Table 2.8.)

We assume that the input price subsidy effectively reduces the price of inputs by 10 percent, so that in the planning stage, farmers plan to use more. (The added amount purchased would be determined by the elasticity of the farmers' demand function for inputs,

Table 2.8. Market Solution for Farm Sector and Two Producer Groups, with an Input Price Subsidy

Item	Solution with Input Subsidy of 10 Percent[a]		
	Market	Large farms	Small farms
Market price	47.80	47.80	47.80
Market quantity	36.0	25.1	10.9
Inputs used	4.93	3.54	1.39
Total farm revenue	1,726.30	1,200.38	526.02
Total farm costs	547.23	392.94	154.29
Net farm revenue	1,179.07	807.34	371.73
Percentage of market net revenue	...	69	31

[a]Compare these magnitudes with those given in Table 2.4 as "original solution." The original solution obtains when no input price support is given.

and is related directly to the production elasticity. In this model, the functions depicting the demand for inputs are elastic with respect to price, so that a decline in price leads to a greater outlay for inputs.) As in the adjustment analysis, we assume that the demand schedule has not changed with economic progress. Likewise, the same production elasticities are retained. New normative supply functions would result, as given in Equations 2.32, 2.33, and 2.34 respectively for the set of large farmers, small farmers, and aggregate market. The market equilibrium magnitudes are those presented in Table 2.8.

$$Q_{s1} = 10 + 35.52P_y P_x^{-1} \tag{2.32}$$

$$Q_{s2} = 5 + 13.9P_y P_x^{-1} \tag{2.33}$$

$$Q_m = 15 + 49.42P_y P_x^{-1} \tag{2.34}$$

The solution to the subsidy-influenced market shows that the relative positions of both sets of farmers in the overall market are roughly the same as before the subsidy was in effect. Even if the subsidy was an actual rebate, the net revenue positions would be the same. This reflects the fact that the subsidy was assumed to be applied to all inputs, those used by both small and large farmers, in the same proportion. This has tended to be the case in Canadian agriculture, at least in the intent of the universal participation programs instituted, such as extension services, credit programs, and so on. If programs were designed to assist low income farmers and used the input subsidy as a means of extending the assistance, it is not likely that the income gap would be closed. If the current model were reestimated with the 10 percent input price reduction accruing only to the inputs used on small farms, the solution under the retained assumptions previously mentioned would show a 68.8/31.2 percent division of income. It is reasonably clear, therefore, that subsidies on the prices of inputs tend not to improve the equity in the distribution of incomes within the sector.

SUBSIDIES PER UNIT OF OUTPUT

In spite of language used to describe a program, a policy instrument is a de facto subsidization of product prices whenever the per unit product price received by the farmer when the program is in effect is higher than that he would get if the price were determined without the program. As in the case of the de facto subsidization of input prices, the farmer need not actually receive a payment to get a subsidized product price. Thus programs which remove uncertainty in the expected product price, such as floor prices or advance payments for grain, and thereby allow the farmer to avoid discounting future expectations when making current production decisions, serve to subsidize the price farmers use as a basis for decision making. As already mentioned in the discussion of supply control, some product marketing boards assist their members in arranging contracts for future product deliveries, practice price discrimination in multimarket selling, and organize product selling by centralizing the activity. Thus their activities within these lines fall into the category of product price support. On a less subtle level, product price subsidization is practiced in Canada by the Canadian Dairy

Commission in its manufactured milk supports and the Agricultural Stabilization Board activities. A list of product price supports is given in Table 2.1. Again, the certainty in the producer's mind about receiving the payment and the frequency with which the payments are made are significant in determining whether the effect of the program will be to put net revenue in the hands of producers or to create the impression in producer's minds that demand is more robust than it is in fact, which leads to surplus accumulation. Obviously, when the program of initial payments to prairie grain growers began, the intent was to pay in advance for the minimum amount of grain that the Canada Wheat Board knew it could market with certainty and subsequently buy more as needed. But when in two or three good selling years, second and third payments became institutionalized, farmers tended to produce and make management decisions based on higher expectations than were reasonable. The consequence has been large carryover stocks and the need for subsequent and supposedly remedial programs. But as long as the farm expectation is high and encouraged, the remedial programs will become institutionalized out of ongoing necessity.

A Model to Evaluate the Adjustment Aspects of the Policy. To illustrate the workings of the product price subsidy mechanism and to measure the impact of this mechanism on the adjustment problem, we reconsider the example given in the first section of this chapter. With an aggregate sectoral production function as in Equation 2.1, and demand as in Equation 2.2, we recall that the market equilibrium situation was described in Table 2.2. (See also Table 2.9.)

Let the product price be subsidized in one of the ways suggested above so that the effective farm price increases, that is

$$P_{y2} = \lambda P_{y1}, \ \lambda > 1$$

This has the effect of increasing the level of demand for inputs and shifts the supply function outward. The new aggregate supply function is Equation 2.35, expressed in preprogram product and input prices.

Table 2.9. Market Solution for Farm Sector, with a Commodity Price Support

Item	Solution with Commodity Price Support of λ Percent[a]
Market price, P	$P_2 = \lambda^{-10/11} P_1 \; (\lambda^{-10/11} < 1)$
Market quantity, Q	$Q_2 = \lambda^{4/11} Q_1 \; (\lambda^{4/11} > 1)$
Inputs used, X	$X_2 = \lambda^{5/11} X_1 \; (\lambda^{5/11} > 1)$
Total farm revenue, TR = P•Q	$TR_2 = \lambda^{-6/11} TR_1 \; (\lambda^{-6/11} < 1)$
Total farm costs, TC = P_x•X	$TC_2 = \lambda^{5/11} TC_1$
Net farm revenue, NR = TR − TC	$NR_2 = \lambda^{-6/11} (1 - 0.8\lambda)(0.2)^{-1} NR_1$

[a]Magnitudes of variables subscripted 1 are given in Table 2.2 as "original solution." Original solution is that obtaining without a commodity price support.

$$Q'_s = \lambda^4 a^5 (0.8)^4 P_x^{-4} P_y^4 \qquad (2.35)$$

Assuming again, as in the last section, that we are interested only in observing the influence of this program type, and not with technical progress, we retain the original demand function, Equation 2.2, and allow the supply function to show only the price-supported shift.

The postpolicy market solution is also given in Table 2.9. The net farm revenue after the subsidy which farmers derive strictly from market operations is less than in the presubsidy case, as is evident from the ratio

$$\frac{NR_2}{NR_1} = \frac{(1 - 0.8\lambda)\ (\lambda^{-6/11})}{(0.2)}$$

which is less than 1 when $\lambda > 1$. This means that the subsidy, if actually paid to the farmer in the form of a cash payment, would first have to compensate the farmer for his losses before it could add to his net income. If no direct payments were made, the subsidy would tax the farm sector for the benefit of the non-farm sector, the latter getting more food at lower per unit costs, while the farmer loses net income.

The economic reasons for this are similar to those which explained the retarded adjustment under a regime of input subsidies. In this case, the upward valuation of the commodity price (rather than the devaluation of input price) in the minds of farmers tends to raise agriculture's holding power on resources already employed in specific enterprises, and tends to make other resources appear more productive. There would be no harm in this if the subsidized output price more closely reflected the true social value of the agricultural commodity than the local market price. This has tended to be the rationale for encouraging agricultural production of specific highly desirable commodities under a spur of subsidies in developing nations and in developed nations in crisis situations, assuming farmers were price motivated.

But in situations where the monetary or other value to society of extra units of agricultural commodities is falling or is negative, the output price subsidy becomes a liability for society as well as the farmer. Clear evidence of this is the Canadian prairie grain situation, in which inventories are growing both because the Canada Wheat Board has given a de facto subsidy to grain prices, and because the Board cannot sell the volume of grains produced under the stimulus. This indicates that the value of more grain in the Canadian west is considerably less than the value set by the Board. The real significance of this, however, is not so much in the accumulation of stocks (which is in fact a nuisance) or in the political bickering surrounding the Board (which is good sport for some), but in the resource misallocation and adjustment retardation which it creates. The significance of misallocation and of retarded adjustment lies in the fact that resources are prevented from earning competitive returns in agriculture, and so farmers earn lower income than would otherwise be possible.

We suggest alternate programs to relieve this problem in Part 2. The programs suggested would tend to accelerate adjustment for the sector, so that resources would generate rising farm incomes, and simultaneously deal with the hardships of individuals through direct means.

A Model to Evaluate the Distributional Aspects of the Policy. In the case of supply control programs, which had the effect of restricting some farmers but not others even though both sets sold their produce in essentially the same market, a differentiated set of benefits accrued. We showed that the policy penalized the controlled farmers when noncontrolled farmers were present. On the other hand, the input price subsidy could not be generally characterized as being for one set of farmers but not another, since it seemed that great administrative difficulty would arise in trying to differentiate the inputs going to use in selected farms. By contrast, the practice of subsidizing output price can readily be interpreted as offering differentiated benefits to farm groups, since the policy is specifically tied to designated outputs, and frequently to the output of specific regions. This would not have constituted a problem if transport technology and food preservation measures had not broadened the size of effective market areas. But with fast communications, futures markets, and transportation advances, arbitrage has been able to spread excess demands and excess supplies over a wider plain.

In Canadian agricultural policy, several programs have the effect of subsidizing the output price of one set of farmers and not that of another. In the livestock industry, for example, Quebec's offering a "quality premium" for hogs while contiguous and accessible provinces do not would tend to enlarge the volume of hogs produced in that province and put downward pressure on the price of hogs in contiguous and accessible markets. This is not to suggest that the subsidizing province would necessarily export hogs to neighboring markets, but only that the presence of the larger supply could permit buyers to be less eager in the markets they normally patronize.

As another example, in the Canadian grain industry, when the Canada Wheat Board offers a de facto price support to prairie-grown grains, the main beneficiary of the supports tends to be wheat, although barley and oats prices are supported to a lesser degree. But because the Board sets delivery quotas which are too low to allow delivery of all wheat grown at the supported price, there is a flow of wheat into the non-Board feed grains markets as competitive grain with nondelivered barley and oats. The non-Board feed markets tend to be localized, since only the Board has the authority to transport grain interprovincially. In effect, subsidized wheat growers and less-well-subsidized feed grains growers come to participate in the same non-Board market. Historically, this market has been volatile, since the variation in Board policy with respect to payments and quotas varies the supply of grain in the non-Board market rapidly, and prices tend to be considerably lower and less stable in this market. Consequently, the barley and oat growers who rely more on the non-Board market as an outlet for their grain and as a source of income, since they do not generally deliver as much to the Board as do wheat growers, suffer income instability because of the spin-off effects of the Board's attempts to raise and stabilize the incomes of wheat growers using price supports.[9]

As a general rule, when two sets of producers with essentially similar production functions, costs, and supply functions sell in the same market (as defined above), the income distribution between them worsens when one group is receiving a de facto price support and the other does not. Moreover, what is more significant is that the nonsubsidized producers tend to become worse off relative to their own former income positions, indicating that the subsidy for the one group of farmers taxes the producers not supported.

This can be demonstrated in a simple model. If there are two producer groups contributing an α share and a β share of the marketed output Q_s, the market,

9. A statistical demonstration of the contrast in degrees of stability of prices in board and nonboard prices is given in T. C. Kerr, An Economic Analysis of the Feed Freight Assistance Policy (Ottawa: Agr. Econ. Res. Council of Canada, 1966), p. 60.

in an equilibrium represented by the original solution in Table 2.2, would distribute income between them in the ratio α/β. This can be readily shown by assuming that

$$Q_s = Q_\alpha + Q_\beta$$

where $\alpha + \beta = 1$ and apportioning inputs, revenue, and costs accordingly; this is possible since we assumed similarity in production functions and costs borne per unit.

When the product price of the α-share producers is supported and the product price of the β-share producers is not, that is,

$$P_{y\alpha 2} = \lambda P_{y\alpha 1} (\lambda > 1)$$

and

$$P_{y\beta 2} = P_{y\beta 1}$$

the normative supply functions for the two groups become Equations 2.36 and 2.37, while the market supply function becomes Equation 2.38. Note that the original market supply function, Equation 2.4, used to get the original solution has shifted outward, but not as far as it did when both producer groups were supported. When $\lambda > 1$, and $\alpha + \beta = 1$, λ^4, the shift in the original to get Equation 2.35, exceeds $\alpha\lambda^4 + \beta$, the shift to get Equation 2.39.

$$Q_{\alpha 2} = \alpha\lambda^4 (0.8)^4 a^5 P_y^4 P_x^{-4} = \alpha\lambda^4 Q_{\alpha 1} \quad (2.36)$$

$$Q_{\beta 2} = \beta (0.8)^4 a^5 P_y^4 P_x^{-4} = \beta Q_{\beta 1} \quad (2.37)$$

$$Q_{s2} = (\alpha\lambda^4 + \beta)(0.8)^4 a^5 P_y^4 P_x^{-4} = (\alpha\lambda^4 + \beta) Q_{s1} \quad (2.38)$$

The market equilibrium solution that results when supply as described in Equation 2.38 interacts with demand as given in Equation 2.2 is presented in Table 2.10. The allotment of the market magnitudes between the two producer groups is also given in Table 2.10.

Table 2.10. Market Solution for Farm Sector and Subgroups in the Sector, When Commodity Price Support Applies to One Group Only

Item	Market Solution with Commodity Price Support of λ Percent[a]	Solution for α-Share Producers (recipients of subsidy)[a]	Solution for β-Share Producers (not recipients of subsidy)[a]
Market price[b]	$P_2 = \delta^{-10/44} P_1 \ (\delta^{-10/44} < 1)$		
Market quantity	$Q_2 = \delta^{1/11} Q_1 \ (\delta^{1/11} > 1)$	$Q_{\alpha 2} = \lambda^4 \alpha \delta^{-10/11} Q_1$	$Q_{\beta 2} = \beta \delta^{-10/11} Q_1$
Inputs used	$X_2 = \delta^{5/44} X_1 \ (\delta^{5/44} > 1)$	$X_{\alpha 2} = \lambda^5 \alpha^{5/4} \delta^{-50/44} X_1$	$X_{\beta 2} = \beta^{5/4} \delta^{-50/44} X_1$
Total farm revenue	$TR_2 = \delta^{-6/11} TR_1$	$TR_{\alpha 2} = \lambda^4 \alpha \delta^{-50/44} TR_1$	$TR_{\beta 2} = \beta \delta^{-50/44} TR_1$
Total farm costs	$TC_2 = \delta^{5/44} TC_1$	$TC_{\alpha 2} = \lambda^9 \alpha^{9/4} \delta^{-90/44} TC_1$	$TC_{\beta 2} = \beta^{9/4} \delta^{-90/44} TC_1$
Net farm revenue[c]	$NR_2 = (1 - \phi) \phi^{-6/11} a^{-30/44} b^{50/44} P_x^{6/11}$	$NR_{\alpha 2} = \rho \lambda^4 \alpha NR_1$	$NR_{\beta 2} = \rho \beta NR_1$

[a]Expressed in terms of original solution given in Table 2.2.

[b]For notational convenience, $\delta = (\alpha\lambda^4 + \beta)$.

[c]For notational convenience, $\phi = 0.8\delta^{1/4}$ and $\rho = 5 \cdot \delta^{-50/44} [1 - \lambda^9 \alpha^{9/4} \delta^{-90/44} (0.8)]$.

The ratio of net revenue of α producers to β producer groups has increased by the factor λ^4, which indicates that the distribution of income between them has worsened. This has occurred because of market forces, not because the government actually paid the α-share producers the amount of the subsidy. If the government did pay the α-group producers, the realized disparity would be even worse. Further, this broader disparity in net income distribution has occurred simultaneously with a decline in total farm sector net revenue.[10] Thus the nonsubsidized producers have fared even less well than in the original solution.

In the list of output price support measures described in Table 2.1, however, the more usual case would be that all farmers receive the subsidy. This would be the case, for example, in a program requiring compulsory participation of all farmers in multipricing marketing board activities. The distribution question when all farmers receive the supported price then revolves around intrasectoral distribution of net income.

The outcome can be investigated with the help of the model presented in the discussion of the distributional outcomes of supply control, in which two producers or producer groups were described, one representing the large scale, the other the small scale operators. The equilibrium values of the market variables in a free market equilibrium are given in Table 2.4. (See Table 2.11.) We assume now that because of some program in which all farmers participate, the realized product price at the farm increases by 10 percent. This means that farmers would use a new product price in their production level calculations which bears the following relation to the old product price:

$$P'_y = 1.1P_y$$

---

10. $NR_2/NR_1 = (1 - \phi)\ \phi^{-6/11}/(1 - 0.8)(0.8)^{-6/11}$. But $(\alpha\ \lambda^4 + \beta) > 1$, so that $\phi > (0.8)$. Thus $(\phi/0.8)^{-6/11} < 1$ and $(1 - \phi)/(1 - 0.8) < 1$. Hence, $NR_2 < NR_1$.

Table 2.11. Market Solution for Farm Sector and Subgroups, with an Output Price Subsidy

Item	Solution with Output Price Subsidy of 10 Percent[a]		
	Market	Large farms	Small farms
Market price	47.60	47.60	47.60
Market quantity	36.21	25.25	10.96
Inputs used	5.06	3.64	1.42
Total farm revenue	1,703.60	1,201.90	521.70
Total farm costs	561.66	404.04	157.62
Net farm revenue	1,161.94	797.86	364.08
Percentage of market net revenue	...	69	31

[a]Compare these magnitudes with those given in Table 2.4 as "original solution." The original solution obtains when no commodity price support is given.

When this occurs, a new supply function results for both sets of farmers and the market as a whole. In terms of old product prices the new supply schedules would be

$$Q_{s1} = 10 + 35.2P_yP_x^{-1} \quad (2.39)$$

$$Q_{s2} = 5 + 13.75P_yP_x^{-1} \quad (2.40)$$

$$Q_m = 15 + 48.95P_yP_x^{-1} \quad (2.41)$$

With no complementary program to restrict supply, increase demand, or subsidize input prices, the increased product offers would meet the demand schedule given by Equation 2.17 and result in a market price in the form of $P = 45P_x(48.95 + 0.5P_x)^{-1}$. (There is no shift in demand, since technological change and economic growth are not admitted into the solution here.) Again, if input prices were represented by $P_x = 111$ as in the preceding applications of the model, the market product would be $P_y = 47.82$. This may not be the actual per unit farm receipt if the program has a money payout provision by the authority involved, but as far as the market can be relied upon to yield revenue, the equilibrium market magnitudes would be those given in Table 2.11.

It is clear from the table that without a direct payment by the authority, the net revenue of both groups of producers would be lower than that earned in the presubsidy market. Also, the distribution of net income between the large and the small farmers after the subsidy program would not be changed. Thus there would be no benefit accruing to the farm sector from such efforts to improve product prices; the quantity of output called forth by the apparently improved price more than frustrated the attempts to improve net income when juxtaposed with inelastic demands for products. Even in the event that a direct payment is made to farmers, net revenue would not be distributed any more equitably than the market, since the production potential of the farms would determine the distribution, just as it did the initial distribution of income. In any event, the direct payment would first have to compensate producers for the loss in net revenue in the market before it could improve previous income distributions.

CONCLUSION

In this chapter we have classified each of the policy instruments typically employed to implement farm programs in Canada into three categories: input subsidies, subsidies per unit of output, and supply management and control activities. We have not evaluated policy instruments designed to enlarge the demand for agricultural products, simply because they are not common and because they do not have side effects that are detrimental to the agricultural sector (see Chap. 8). In each case we have shown the influences of the mechanisms on (1) the adjustment problem as seen in the farm-nonfarm income disparity, and (2) the intrasectoral income distribution.

In no case did the mechanisms help to close the intrasectoral income gap, and in the case of supply restrictions activity, the gap may actually be widened, depending on the method of administering quotas. This indicates that no mechanism has the power to improve the lot of the poor farmer relative to the wealthier farmer.

The mechanisms exhibit differing impacts on the farm-nonfarm income gap, and by implication, the pace of agricultural adjustment. Supply control could keep the intersectoral income gap closed under certain conditions which could be met in Canada. Subsidies per unit of input could have either positive or negative effects on the intersectoral income gap, depending upon the elasticities of demand and supply, but it is unlikely that the conditions could be met in Canada in the future. Subsidies per unit of output effectively tax the farm sector and widen the intersectoral income gap.

Hence, if agricultural adjustment and an improvement in intrasectoral income distribution is to be part of the objective of national agricultural policy, a discrete break with traditional methods of extending assistance must be made, and new means of transferring wealth found.

We suggest normatively that closing the income gaps ought to be part of a new agricultural policy, and so we will suggest new means of wealth transfer in Part 2.

3 Political Failure of Canadian Agricultural Policy

THE HISTORY of Canadian agricultural policy reveals that Canadian farmers have been willing to form voluntary organizations in the attempt to realize their goals. The history of cooperative wheat marketing in western Canada in the 1920s and the attempts to form marketing boards during the 1930s are part of the evidence of this fact.

Equally revealing in Canadian agricultural history is the laissez-faire attitude pervading government (particularly federal government) policy with respect to the agricultural sector. The slowness of government to respond to the agricultural population's needs generated by the depression (and there is some doubt that it was the depression-generated needs that the government responded to), and the apparent reluctance to get involved in a permanent way illustrated the attitude. When the government did act, it tended to respond to pressure, waiting for the policy need to be articulated elsewhere in the farm community before acting, and then apparently acting only to meet the need as articulated. It has adopted a passive, reluctant leadership style rather than assuming the role as director of policy.

One must be cautious in making such a generalization about government's approach, however, since many programs have shown foresight and long-range planning (for example, the planning for the war-to-peace transition of agriculture). But when active federal leadership has been given to agriculture it has tended to be because other national objectives required the resources and output of the agricultural sector.

It is not intended that this be a criticism of the

leadership style, for certainly it is the leadership style which appears to be most consistent with the presumably independent, individualistic character of farm operators, as well as liberal democratic idealism. Rather, it suggests that the passive (if responsive) form of government leadership permits the creation of an agricultural policy characterized by a specific regional, commodity-oriented, "pork-barrel" set of internally inconsistent measures. This has been the case in United States agricultural policy as well as in Canadian. It is the purpose of the following sections to show that the style of leadership of Canadian federal governments in the past has complemented the development of the policy mechanisms that we have shown to be ineffective in dealing with agriculture's fundamental problems.

PROCESS OF SOCIAL ACTION

"Success" can be thought of as having reached a goal. Goals can be long term in nature or short term. Short-term objectives are often stepping-stones on a path leading to longer-term goals, the path being determined, in part, by what the party involved perceives to be the long-term cause-and-effect relationships of the actual situation.

In the preceding chapters we have suggested that success in achieving short-term goals such as a supported price of a commodity, a subsidized price for production inputs, or a reduced offering of commodity in markets in no way guarantees the attainment of the longer-term or broader goal of farm income and welfare improvement. Yet these short-term, or narrow, successes have historically been what farm groups have organized to achieve. Further, this is what has been granted by government.

This situation has probably evolved, in part, not because thinkers were generally ignorant of the relationships shown above, but because it was easier to achieve success in narrow, short-term, commodity-oriented goals than in programs requiring a more abstract level of problem perception. In fact, given the nature of volunteer organizations, success itself tends to become a goal, regardless of the direction in which the success leads. The truth of this situation is made clear in considering the process through which an organization typically goes in holding itself together and achieving a success. The organization may not consciously go through each of the steps in the process described below, or even go through these steps in the order given; but that does not invalidate the analysis. The significance of the analysis lies in the fact that through a delineation of the process the analyst can obtain a feeling for the evolution of social action, and more clearly pinpoint the causes of the failure of Canadian farm groups in solving their fundamental problems politically.

The Single Group

To illustrate what is involved in the process of social action we use a hypothetical example.[1] The example could typify one or other of the many cases in which plans were made during the depression for producer marketing boards. At first it might appear that our argument could be strengthened if the history of a specific board were considered for illustrative purposes. But because much of the process of social action is conducted informally in nondocumented (nondocumentable) person-to-person contact, an actual history would not add significantly to this exposition. We are content, therefore, to let the following argument stand as a hypothesis about the probable course of events in a Canadian setting. The hypothesis has some support in that (1) some groups in Canada have been successful in achieving goals like obtaining subsidies and restricting output and (2) it has been shown elsewhere that a set of steps does exist which increases the probability of success in achieving goals.

It should be clear that the purpose is not to condemn nor advocate the activities of any marketing board or farm volunteer organization in this exposition. If any moral judgments are implied, they are

1. Much of the theory underlying this discussion is drawn from work done over the past two decades by J. M. Bohlen, G. M. Beal, and others, primarily at Iowa State University, Ames. Specific references will be made as needed below.

concerned with the policy stance of government. Obviously, private individuals, as self-seekers, are fully justified in presenting their positions to government. Government, on the other hand, is the only agent in national economic life with the power and the point of view to determine what is best for the nation, including both present and future generations. Government is indeed the referee among individuals and their organizations. If government does not force self-seeking individuals to compromise, then it is probably the fault of the government, not the self-seeking individuals if results are found to be unsatisfactory.

In the case of a marketing board, a long-term goal might have been defined in which mitigating the decline in net income was an objective. To do this, the short-term goal or the "means to the end" could be to organize a compulsory board empowered to restrict the supply of products entering organized markets, raise commodity prices, and administer a quota system so that producers could share the benefits of the action.

By suggesting this as a strategy, the farmers involved in the initial planning stages would have completed the "convergence of interest."[2] This suggests that several individual or social instigators may have decided to act in unison, after perceiving that they had a common problem (their loss of real income). They would have made a tentative appraisal of the cause of their problem and hence they would hypothesize a solution. As previously discussed in Chapter 1, their rea-

---

2. The sociological definitions of this and subsequent terms have been given and explained with the following literature: George M. Beal and Joe M. Bohlen. The Group Process, Instructors Guide, Communication Training Program, Am. Assoc. of Land Grant Colleges, National Project in Agricultural Communication, East Lansing, Mich., 1956—the first formal articulation of this particular model of social action; George M. Beal, How Does Social Change Occur? Cooperative Ext. Serv. RS-284, Iowa State Univ., Ames, 1958; George M. Beal and Harold R. Capener, A Social Action Model, a paper presented at the Rural Sociology Meeting, Pullman, Washington, 1958; George M. Beal, Social Action: Instigated Social Change in Large Social Systems, in Our Changing Rural Society, edited by James H. Copp (Ames: Iowa State Univ. Press, 1964); George M. Beal and Daryl J. Hobbs, The Process of Social Action in Community and Area Development, Cooperative Ext. Serv. Soc-16, Iowa State Univ., Ames, August 1969.

soning might be as follows: The price level for a given commodity is too low to give a high enough net farm income after expenses are paid. Facing a demand for food which is price inelastic, producers could withhold the product from the market, thereby raising the product's price and increasing total revenue to farmers as a body. The increased total revenue could be alloted among producers by assigning each producer either a production or delivery quota. Simultaneously, the lower output would require lower inputs so that a decline in total cost could result. The joint effects of these changes would be a rise in net farm income.

Whether or not this theory of the cause and effect of the problem is correct (which it could be for producers as a whole) is not important for this analysis. What is important is that after this initial convergence of interest among a few concerned persons, they decide to act.

Once the decision to act has been made by the initial instigators, three planning steps would typically be taken. These steps would involve an "analysis of the prior social situation," an "analysis of the existing social system," and a "delineation of the relevant social system."[3]

The instigators might try to learn about what experiences farmers had in the past with organizing boards for collective marketing (and about the prairie grain marketing efforts in the 1920s), what successes were gained, what failures and why, and whether farmer self-help through cooperative marketing could be generally accepted by producers. This may be done by survey, attending meetings, or other intelligence gathering means. Then they might evaluate the current situation, learning whether there were legal restrictions on their proposed activity, suggesting which individuals or groups might best be included in the proposed scheme to make it most successful, what politicians could be influenced using what means, and examining the most feasible, yet permissible, boundaries (geographic) to their scheme. Lastly, the instigators would try

3. Designated as steps 2, 1, and 4 respectively in Beal and Hobbs, Process of Social Action, pp. 3-4.

to identify the relevant social system for the future formation and operation of the plan. This would identify those who would be the targets of the proposed action. In doing this, they would have their own concept of the causal relationships involved in the problem in mind; hence, they would probably identify as "relevant" all the producers of the same commodity in a geographic area and the interactions between these producers and government. They could not expect that the producers of beef, for example, would be at all concerned about the limits placed on the supply of beans entering the bean market.

With the first round of planning essentially completed, a link[4] would be established by the instigators with those "powerful" individuals who could either encourage the plan and lend their support to it or effectively kill it. This step of "legitimation"[5] is vital in any social action movement, for it is in this process that the plan of the instigators is confronted by the interests of the relevant power structure, the de facto leadership of these elements of society with an interest in the commodity. Obviously, no action begins in a political vacuum, so that any new political action would eventually come to cross swords with "the establishment." The establishment would have its own set of goals and would only legitimize, or permit to operate, those movements which would not seriously harm them. At this point the producer organization, as planned for, would not yet exist; hence, positional leaders would probably not exist, so that formal legitimation would not be possible. (The formal legitimation in the form of governmental authorization to conduct activity as a compulsory marketing board is not considered here, since that is the goal sought.) Even so it would undoubtedly be known to the instigators that the support of certain individuals (informal legitimizers) within the relevant social system would insure success. These could grant a "license to act."[6]

Recognizing the fact that informal legitimation is

---

4. Ibid., "Initiating set," step 4, p. 5.

5. Ibid., step 5, p. 5.

6. Beal, How Does Social Change Occur? pp. 30-31.

necessary merely acknowledges that in any political system there are persons with power who can help or hinder the plans of those instigating change. The importance of this is that once a plan is legitimized it has a chance of becoming a reality. Canada, of course, has an informal power structure which could and has legitimized actions.[7]

In cases involving legislation, the formal and informal leadership would undoubtedly include representatives of political parties and government personnel. In the process of legitimation, the leadership could challenge the plan and force modifications. Most of the compromises would be reached, and new information drawn from wider spheres of interest brought into contact or conflict with the instigators' plan. This would be the stage at which the original theory of the instigators concerning the causal relationships affiliated with their perceived problem would be tested and rejected if false.

Once legitimized, the plan would have large elements of the power structure behind it, and the likelihood of changing the original concepts at a later stage would decrease sharply. Once the plan is legitimized properly, the instigators would have a high degree of confidence that when a producers' group was formed and requested the powers of a compulsory, regional, one-commodity marketing board, the government would pass the appropriate legislation to grant the power.

At this point the few who had been associated with the plan in the inception stage would come out from behind the scenes and openly work for the success of their plan. The process from this point on is more or less straightforward. This is the point at which a chronological history of the movement would begin.

The instigators would diffuse their idea and plan throughout the relevant social system, probably the producers of the commodity involved. This would require resources—financial, personal (leadership), and

---

7. See John Porter, The Vertical Mosaic, Pt. 2 (Toronto: Univ. of Toronto Press, 1968), in which Canada's power structure is analyzed with the "power elite" model, pp. 201-30 ff.

organizational. In the example under consideration, these resources would probably be used to plan the appropriate appeals to the producers of the commodity involved (the predecided target group). The resources might be used to draw farmers together into a constituted group and, through "solicitation or propaganda," to help producers in general to see the problem perceived by the instigators as their problem, and the legitimized solution as the right solution.

The instigators would, in the parlance of social action theory, develop their "diffusion sets" in order to "define the need"[8] in the relevant social system (the farmers of the commodity involved).

Having done this, the instigators would seek a "commitment to action" by the producers involved. In the example used here, this would be the actual formation of the group to present the demand that the power of a compulsory marketing board be given by government to them. They would then have formulated their objectives and presented them in the form of a constitution or charter and decided on the means they wished to use to restrict supply. Now they would plan their approach to government and mobilize the resources needed to actively effect the passage of the necessary legislation.[9]

Summary. The process which we assumed to be a necessary precondition for the success of an instigated social action involves two distinct phases. The first involves the essentially nonpublicized, but not necessarily secretive, process of planning and compromising among those comprising the group of concerned activists, and between this group and the relevant formal or informal power structure. The second phase involves what the instigators themselves would hope to be a well-publicized open action to form cohesive organizations for the purpose of achieving previously determined goals through previously planned means.

In the nonpublic phase (the first phase) the most significant decisions concerning all future actions

---

8. Beal and Hobbs, Process of Social Action, steps 7 and 8, p. 7.

9. Ibid., steps 9-14, pp. 11-14.

are set, for it is in this phase that the instigators decide what causal relationships are relevant and what individuals need to be involved (the relevant social system) in the public phase. It is in the nonpublic phase that legitimation occurs, and any conflicts between the desires of the instigators and the desires of the power structure are worked out. By the time public attention is drawn to a movement, its essential philosophy is fixed. Any debate or compromise occurring in the second or public phase would be conducted within the boundaries already set by this basic philosophy. In the example used in the preceding section, this is interpreted as meaning that initially a set of instigators decided that the income problem could be solved by means of a compulsory commodity marketing board which could restrict the flow of output into markets. This theory must have been legitimized in the sense that those powerful individuals who could have either killed the notion or changed it did not. Hence, when producers actually formed the boards (the public action), debate would only revolve around matters such as officers, timing, quantities offered, quota distribution, and so on. But no debate would be held concerning whether or not the board itself should survive.

One might object at this point that the example used is not consistent with the social action hypothesis, since the Supreme Court of Canada found the legislation allowing the formation of compulsory producer marketing boards in the 1930s ultra vires, or beyond the legal authority of the provincial governments. But the reenactment of permissive legislation after World War II really demonstrates that the concept of the compulsory marketing board was properly legitimized even in the 1930s. The failure to receive legal sanction in the 1930s merely shows that the parties to the action failed to take all the critical elements in the existing social system of the day into account (the critical element here being the question of federal-provincial jurisdiction as it was seen to apply to trade).

SIGNIFICANCE OF THIS ANALYSIS

Is this type of reasoning relevant to the problem of analyzing the history of Canada's agricultural policy? Even more important, is it relevant to the problem of suggesting new policy guidelines? The answer to the second question is affirmative; and the contribution of this understanding will be made clear in Part 2 of this book. To answer the first question, we have indicated that an understanding of the process of social change, even when stated in terms abstracted from a concrete case, helps to precisely identify the social, or rather the political, root of the failure of Canadian agricultural policy in actually solving the fundamental problems of the sector.

Consider the initial convergence of interest of several individuals. The convergence occurred because there was perceived commonality among the initial planners. The most obvious ways in which persons perceived commonality among themselves would be exploited first as a basis for convergence. For example, sameness of enterprises, market outlet, locale, in addition to the belief concerning the problem and the way to solve it, would be relevant. Convergence would appear to be stronger the more things producers found in common, provided they were relevant to the perceived problem. In addition, when the individuals thought about the boundaries which would define the relevant social system in their proposed solution they would begin by including those who shared their own common characteristics, and excluding those who had fewer things in common with them. Hence, one would not expect dairymen and cash crop producers to freely unite, nor would one expect to find cattlemen and poultrymen naturally forming a convergence of interest when dealing with agricultural income problems. In fact, one can observe even within the "farmers' unions" that have developed in Canada within the past few years, the existence of commodity cliques whose members owe prime allegiance to the clique rather than to the union (a conclusion based on personal contacts of the authors with individuals in responsible positions in the unions).

Thus we conclude that when farm groups were able to define the social system in which they wished to work without any restrictions or guidance, they tended toward the formation of commodity-oriented groups. As long as they are free to do so in the future, the most powerful farm groups will tend first to form along commodity lines.

During the course of prewar Canadian agricultural history there had been little indication that farm groups were not acting in their own best interests by concentrating their activity on solving the problems associated with specific commodities in hopes of improving their own welfare. Hence, when a postwar group of instigators would evaluate prior experience and analyze their current social situation, there would be no clear evidence to suggest an alternate, noncommodity approach. Without restrictions or guidance to the contrary, farmers would continue to think along commodity lines when making tentative plans and would seek legitimation for commodity programs.

As indicated in the preceding section, the first point at which instigators' plans are subjected to serious scrutiny by anyone outside the instigators' intimate group comes in the stage of legitimation. If the formal or informal leadership of the relevant power structure challenges the logic or the intent of the proposed plan in light of their own broader interests then the plan will be modified or dropped.

This is effectively the last stage in social action at which new or outside information can be added, shortsightedness or narrowness removed, and the fundamental causal relationships and philosophy of the plan clarified. After legitimation the plan probably has the support of the power structure and can proceed in the open.

Because of this, the legitimizer must assume the role of a referee. The role will be played in a way which is consistent with the legitimizer's philosophy. If the process required the legitimation of members of political parties or the civil service, as it would in the case of a proposed enactment or change in legislation, then the prevailing political philosophy of the day would influence the degree to which the referee's role was directive as opposed to laissez-faire.

It has been shown in Chapter 1 that Canadian political attitude had been more or less passive with respect to agriculture, except when national objectives demanded otherwise. Thus, we hypothesize that, as legitimizers, party and governmental personnel would have been nondirective at the time legitimation for currently surviving programs was sought, not seriously challenging the stated wishes of the farm groups. This may have reflected a desire for political support among the rural population on the part of political aspirants, or other social and economic considerations. However, legitimation of commodity programs did occur, and farm groups were not forced to take account of the type of reasoning which claims that the causal relationships between commodity programs and realized net farm income were, at best, weak. Over time it has been deemed necessary for political survival not to disturb the commodity-oriented institutions, but now, with voting power shifting increasingly away from agricultural regions, this may no longer be as necessary as it was. A suggested new perspective on farm groups and government's relationship with them is given in Chapter 7.

We see the relevance of the sociological analysis given in the preceding section. It is useful in pointing out that, left completely to their own devices, genuinely concerned individuals in the farm sector would tend to form commodity-oriented interest groups and seek narrow commodity-oriented programs as the solution to their perceived problems. In Canada in the 1930s they would have observed situations in which such action had been effective at least in a very short-run sense and would not have been constrained either by the existing social structure (laws, attitudes, and customs) or legitimizers from seeking commodity goals.

In the postwar period, legitimation still failed to challenge the assumed positive causal relationships between commodity manipulation and net farm income fundamental to the commodity programs which developed. In essence, those who could have (and in our judgment should have) legitimized an entirely different type of farm program permitted the farm groups to make an error in their reasoning.

In Part 2 we suggest what would constitute a more desirable agricultural policy for Canada in the coming decade and beyond. We further suggest means through which a change in government leadership style might be affected and indicate the ways in which this would facilitate the implementation of the programs recommended.

2 A PRESCRIPTION FOR THE FUTURE

4 Direction of a New Agricultural Policy

THE EVIDENCE presented in Part 1 showed that Canada's greatest need in agriculture is for policies aimed at solving those problems of the sector created by the general economic phenomena of growth in production capacity, of structural transformation, of the tendency for poverty and low real incomes to be perpetuated within regions and among particular groups of people, and of the competitive nature of agricultural firms.

The history of Canadian agricultural policy has shown itself to be to a large extent a "jerry-built" structure with a foundation of commodity programs with additions tacked on as other specific problems arose. Yet the evidence in Chapter 1 showed that the policy mechanisms built on input and commodity programs have been unable to overcome the initial inequities inherent in agriculture. Policies and programs have continued to allow greater gains to some regions over others, greater advantages to larger farmers with consequent disregard for smaller, and even greater gains to producers of particular commodities in some provinces at a sacrifice to producers of the same commodity in other provinces.

Commodity programs have been shown to have characteristics which can intensify the rate of structural transformation and speed the rate at which people are forced to withdraw from agriculture. But when they have withdrawn they have typically been forced to sell their assets at discounted prices or to migrate into the urban sector where they compete at a disadvantage. This is because commodity programs tend to reward those who stay in agriculture and operate on an ever larger scale while doing nothing for those who must leave both the industry and their communities. In addition, it has been shown that commodity programs often worsen the position of the truly low income families concentrated in agriculture relative to richer farm families.

Similarly, commodity-based policies do not deal with the broader and deeper problems of the rural community to which the changing structure of the sector gives rise: erosion of the rural community, which causes a decay in the trade, capital values, and returns to skills, businesses, and institutions in the country towns.

This all occurs because the instruments typically used in the implementation of commodity programs have been too indirect, so that the full impact of public outlays does not reach the farm families for which they were intended. The beneficial impacts tend to become (1) directed into support for transportation and storage facilities; (2) diverted to the food-processing sector as it becomes integrated with farming; (3) passed on to the consumer because of the competitive nature of farming and the market sector; or (4) (even when the above forces do not divert subsidies from the farmer's hands) capitalized into farm asset values. These will always be the results where public policies rest on commodity and input programs, particularly if the public outlay is fed into the economic system not directly to the farm family. The phenomenon is exaggerated where the industry is extremely competitive, has an oversupply of human and real estate resources, is attached to a sufficiently competitive market sector, possesses extreme immobility of certain labor and capital resources, and is faced with commodity demands of low elasticity.

This is not to deny that some broad commodity programs have brought important gains to agriculture. Wheat board programs which have stabilized the marketing and price of food wheat and have been influential in expanding foreign demand for this commodity should be mentioned. Similarly, per unit dairy subsidies have put extra funds into the hands of many poor farmers, although they have done little to solve the basic problems of large supply capacity and an unfavorable demand situation for the products subsidized. Even so, attempts to solve the problems of agriculture as embodied in these specific commodities have tended only to shift the instability to other competitive commodity groups. The need is for a discrete change in policy emphasis and an approach that recognizes the basic income problem of agriculture as something different from a commodity's price or that price's stability, or input supply-demand imbalances, and that presents solutions which attack the income problem directly.

QUANTITATIVE AND QUALITATIVE POLICY CHANGE

Since the early 1950s when Tinbergen and others presented a theory (and operational basis) of quantitative economic policy making, planners have made a distinction between qualitative economic policy changes and quantitative economic policy changes.[1]

In the sphere of agricultural policy, for example, changes in the size of the initial payment to grain growers, the number of bushels per acre of grain delivered to the Canada Wheat Board, or the price paid per pound of butterfat by milk marketing boards represent quantitative policy changes. Obviously these quantitative policy changes are made by the directors of the programs as they try to achieve some target, such as a desired gross income level, for those in whose interest the policy was presumably made. But one of the implied assumptions behind the belief that the prescribed quantitative policy change will actually lead to achieving the target is that the fundamental structure of the subeconomy involved has not changed over time: that is, what was previously conceived of as a model of the sector still reflects the true situation in the sector. The belief that a quantitative policy change will be successful also assumes that the policy maker has a well-specified and reasonably well-

1. Among the literature outlining parts of the theory is included: Earl O. Heady, ed., Economic Models and Quantitative Methods for Decisions and Planning in Agriculture (Ames, Iowa State Univ. Press, 1971); Jan Tinbergen, On the Theory of Economic Policy (Amsterdam: North Holland Publ. Co., 1952); Jan Tinbergen, The Design of Development (Baltimore: Johns Hopkins Press, 1958); Henri Theil, Optimal Decision Rules for Government and Industry (Amsterdam: North Holland Publ. Co., 1966).

quantified set of relationships describing the system with which he is working. To be successful, the quantitative policy-making process requires that targets (goals) not only be specified qualitatively, but quantified. Hence it is not enough to say that net farm income should be higher; one would also have to say by how much. Finally, to be successful, there must be a real logical and workable link between the goal and the means at the disposal of the policy maker (the instrument) for achieving the goal.

Stated in this context, one can see again why Canadian agricultural policy has failed to solve its income and adjustment problems to date. None of the four essential conditions for the success of a quantitative policy have been met historically. The fundamental qualitative structure of the agricultural (and agribusiness) sector has yet to be specified, let alone quantified, although work is currently under way to do this.[2] Further, there have been rapid changes in the structure of agriculture, spurred in part by the policies actually enforced in the past. Third, as shown in Chapter 2, there has not been a consistently logical link between the goals of improved net income and greater resource mobility and the basic instruments used in Canadian agricultural policies (input subsidies, output subsidies, and supply restraints). Lastly, even the goals themselves have not been stated quantitatively, although some discussion of what might constitute a set of goals has been undertaken.[3]

Qualitative policy changes, in contrast with quantitative policy changes, would be appropriately rec-

---

2. At the time of writing, the authors are aware of three such efforts. The first is the input-output modeling conducted by the Dominion Bureau of Statistics based on 1961 data and updated for certain regions and sectors to a 1965 base. The second is a linear program treatment of the Canadian grain production sector: W. J. Craddock, Interregional Competition in Canadian Cereal Production, Econ. Council of Canada, Spec. Rept. 12, March 1970. A third analysis of both livestock and grain economics in a linear programming framework is underway in the Canadian Dept. of Agr. (Regina office).

3. See, for example, Federal Task Force on Agriculture, Canadian Agriculture in the Seventies (Ottawa: Queen's Printer, 1970). See especially Chap. 3 and the recommendation that these goals be defined.

ommended if there were a need of new policy instruments in light of perceived structural change, and recognized logical links between newly imagined instruments and targets. Qualitative changes would also be involved if there were a restatement of goals.

Much has been said recently in Canada about "pyramids of goals" in the agricultural sector;[4] perhaps too much has been said. In an effort to be clear and all inclusive, the discussions have ranged over macro-level national agricultural goals and micro-level goals dealing with specific inputs, outputs, and regions. This proliferation gives the impression (possibly unintentionally) that specific policies could or ought to be developed simultaneously for each separate goal. This is a mistake, for the interdependence between micro-level goals and macro-level goals means that both cannot be sought simultaneously with complete freedom of choice. The problem is to identify the direction of causality in the relationship between them.

As indicated in Chapter 3, social systems among farm groups in Canada have tended to insure success in achieving such micro-level goals as stabilizing commodity prices or restricting the marketed supply of commodities, in the mistaken belief that attaining these micro-level goals guaranteed macro-level goals such as adequate net farm incomes relative to nonfarm incomes, or a decrease in sectoral income disparities. This indicates a belief that the direction of causation in the "pyramid" is from the bottom up. This attitude has been perpetuated generally in policy discussions. But history has shown this reasoning to be incorrect.

The more appropriate causal relationship is "from the top down." A policy specifically designed for, and directly applied to, the achieving of a macro-level goal will either simultaneously achieve or preclude the need for the micro-level goals previously

4. Ibid., Chap. 3; or A. M. McCalla, A Review and Appraisal of Agricultural Policies in Canada, a paper presented to the Thirteenth Annual Workshop of the Canadian Agricultural Economics Society, Univ. of Guelph, Guelph, Ontario, 1968.

designated as separate (if programs of implementation are administered correctly). In aiming to attain a macro-level goal, one would need only to insure that problems at more micro levels do not frustrate the chances of attaining the macro-level goal.

Specifically, the arguments outlined in Part 1 lead to the conclusion that subsidies paid in the support of farm commodity prices are not generally effective in achieving equity between the welfare of farm and nonfarm families, or between relatively well-to-do and poverty level farmers. Programs at the micro level do not achieve the macro-level objective of equity. But if low income farmers or farmers in general participated in a direct income supplementation scheme for example (the macro-level program), policy makers would not have to continue supporting the commodity price level for these purposes. Price levels could be supported if, for example, added incentive to produce a specific commodity were deemed necessary, but supports would then be an instrument of positive supply management. They would complement direct income support, being aimed at removing a bottleneck which could adversely effect real net income, because the program would alleviate a threat of inflation.

For the remainder of this book, emphasis will be placed on policies to attain the macro-level goals that have received some public support elsewhere in Canada. These support farm incomes at a level comparable to incomes in the nonfarm sector by attaining the goals of greater resource mobility and freedom of adjustment in the agricultural sector, and eventually alleviate rural poverty through compensation. The policy instruments proposed will be directed toward these goals and will represent a qualitative break with historical instruments.

A PREVIEW OF PART 2

The main programs outlined in the following chapters of Part 2 are aimed at resolving the basic and fundamental economic problems of agriculture. They are commodity-free programs in that they deal with problems of farmers in general, but they are designed specifically for the fundamental problems that exist and are without a solution even today. The main elements would substitute for part of the piecemeal complex of commodity and indirect programs that have proved to be inefficient means for attaining the goals of income support and equity because they have been so highly ineffective in solving the underlying problems of adjustment and rural poverty. The suggested policies would largely eliminate the need for a complicated set of programs specified for individual commodities. Therefore, in the following sections we include only those commodity programs which are related to the unique problems of the commodities themselves, such as their tendency to be in cyclical and excess supply and so on, and which in this way are removed from the complex of general problems of the transformation of the farm structure and chronic low income.

On one hand the programs outlined rely heavily on the free market mechanism in determining the production and pricing of commodities. The role of the market in determining the amount of each commodity produced relative to others, the location of production, and interregional commodity movements, as well as making similar decisions would be increased from the system as it now works. Production would be guided more by market demand with the elimination of marketing quotas and subsidies, and by the prices of inputs as determined by their true alternative uses.

However, public policy, rather than the market, would have more influence in other directions. The public would intervene more directly to determine the distribution and levels of net incomes by directing income supplements to both commercial and noncommercial farmers so as to close income and welfare gaps. This would provide greater assurance that public subsidies would come to rest in the hands of farm families. Public policy would also play a larger role in setting standards of income and providing a minimum income for poor families, in salvaging and developing the abilities and potentials of people being forced out of agriculture, and in solving the problems of the rural nonfarm community. Of course, the market mechanism might well be expected to solve all these latter problems in fifty years or so. But in the meantime the lives, capacities, and welfare of many persons in farming would be wasted and many rural communities would suffer almost total disruption. Hardship for people caught in a changing farm world would be perpetuated, not alleviated.

Thus the programs suggested here place greater reliance on the marketplace in the case of commodities and less reliance on it when dealing with families, communities, and social problems. The programs, therefore, would be most consistent with the dual national goals of equity, growth, and stability in human welfare, and economic efficiency in production.

There has been growing recognition in Canada that there are two types of farming operations and operators—those that are viable in a market economy and those that are not, and that two distinct types of policies are needed. For example, in 1969 a policy statement made to the Canadian Outlook Conference in Ottawa by the Agricultural Institute of Canada stated in part that to attain the twin goals of maximizing efficient physical resource utilization and maximizing the well-being of farm people, governments would need to recognize "that in agriculture as in other areas, there are some families whose assets are such that an adequate level of income can only be supplied by welfare. . . ."

More recently the Federal Task Force on Agriculture suggested: "Programs which try to serve the interests of commercial farmers and to meet the problems of poverty-level farmers are unlikely to be successful as separate (but coordinated) programs designed to serve each. . . . The government should not confuse economic and welfare problems and programs to overcome each."[5]

The level of assets or of income which separates these two classes will of course vary from region to region, enterprise to enterprise, and farm to farm. Although some guideline might be appropriate for the separation of the two, as a general rule (based on

---

5. Federal Task Force, Canadian Agriculture in the Seventies, recommendation 4, p. 301.

what can reasonably be forecast about the changes in structure, market conditions, production technology, etc.) no hard and fast rule needs to be drawn for the sake of operational national policy. Specification of even general guidelines might proceed more along the lines of defining personal character profiles of farmers than of impersonal farm analysis, even though the two are related.[6]

In the final analysis the farmer himself ought to be allowed to decide upon his own status. Of course, having opted for one status, he would be expected to be satisfied with the outcomes of his choice. If the choice were made with the assistance of extension counsellors or other agents, this condition would not create difficulties. As of November 1970, Canadian Farm Management Data System (CANFARM), a federal organization designed to computerize farm accounts records and supply auxiliary farm management services, provided monthly and annual financial and production reports based on data collected for about 4,200 Canadian farms. Operating on a nationwide basis, such organizations as CANFARM or Agricultural and Rural Development Association (ARDA) could help farmers explore what changes would be needed to retain viability over a reasonable time into the future, and discover whether adjustment within the sector were even feasible, an activity already engaged in by ARDA in some provinces.

In the following chapters, programs are suggested for both commercial and noncommercial farmers. The programs attempt to provide the means of immediate adjustment and relief for noncommercial farmers, and the means of ongoing adjustment for commercial farmers. These measures could be frustrated if many existing policy instruments were retained, so that the programs include the phased removal of some of the typical policy instruments of Canadian agriculture. Lastly, the potential of Canadian agriculture to become increasingly productive is recognized as a threat to the use-

---

6. See as an example the eight typologies suggested by W. James White, Guidelines for Adjustment; A Blueprint for Progress, A.I.C. Rev. 24 (July-Aug. 1969):8.

fulness of the income policies in actually solving the income problems of the sector; hence, supply management programs are suggested. Even in this a departure is made from the traditional mechanisms that have been shown to be ineffective as distribution-improving tools.

Wherever possible, the existing institutional structure of Canadian agriculture has been viewed as the best means of implementing the revised programs. In this way the recommendations are more for the realignment of existing agricultural policy machinery, rather than for its destruction and re-creation.

5 An Income Policy for Commercial Farmers

BECAUSE the policy mechanisms employed in the past in an attempt to improve real net farm incomes have failed to achieve that goal, it is important to make such an effort again using different means. This would only be consistent with current Canadian beliefs in a degree of equity in the distribution of income.

In the long run, one would hope and expect that the share of national income accruing to an individual in agricultural employment would be roughly proportional to his contribution to national wealth, material or otherwise, as valued in the market. But in the short run, one might have to accept that a transfer of income to specific individuals, of what might be considered a disproportionately large amount is necessary to allow them to reach socially desirable living standards.

The relatively low earning capacity of resources when committed to agricultural production rather than nonfarm production is an accepted piece of traditional wisdom and is generally true considering the existing structure of the sector. Resources once committed to agricultural production tend to become fixed in sectoral use, because the costs involved in intersector resource movement would exceed the expected difference in earnings. Because of a tendency toward rising costs per unit of output, and prices which rise at a slower rate (if at all in real terms), a farm operator must expand to maintain his real net income, and to protect the value of his previous investments. As has been pointed out this does not suggest that all farmers are truly "underpaid" even though their absolute dollar return appears low in relation to wages in the nonfarm sector (living costs and conditions not taken into account).[1] Rather, it suggests that if resources in the sector were somehow reorganized, if some farmers left the sector, and if policies which freeze the agricultural sector in its present structure were abandoned, incomes could eventually be earned by entrepreneurs in agriculture comparable to those earned in the nonfarm sectors by those of comparable abilities.

But there is a time period over which structural adjustment of the agricultural sector would occur. Hence, an adequate policy prescription should contain short-term (transitional) programs which would eventually phase out into long-term (permanent) programs. Desirable income and living levels which may be market earned in the longer run might best be provided by direct income support in the short run.

In addition to the desirability of a direct income policy because it appears to be morally right, there is a need for public policy to attempt to insure ongoing stability of income for the farm families who remain in the sector even after "adjustment" has occurred. The need for stabilization policies has long been recognized because of the nature of production cycles, weather variation, market fluctuations, and so on. However, in the past it has been price stability that was sought, not necessarily income stability.

Stability in this sense does not mean "pegged" or constant income, but rather implies that a farm family could have a high degree of confidence in maintaining the level of real income that they currently enjoy. In a sense this is currently Canadian national policy with respect to the nonfarm population, the attitude being embodied in unemployment insurance schemes, welfare programs, medicare, and so on.

To clarify a second point, it cannot be assumed that adjustment is a once-and-for-all occurrence. The specific adjustment, seen here as occurring in the transitional stage, would be severe and a product of special government action. After this period there would still be adjustment in agriculture as new en-

---

1. See B. B. Perkins, Are Farmers Underpaid? Mimeograph paper, Univ. of Guelph, Guelph, Ontario, 1965.

trants come into the sector, as others retire, as new technological advances are incorporated in production, as new scale economies and diseconomies are discovered, and as tastes and preferences change in consuming sectors. But in posttransitional agriculture such adjustments would occur between fewer farms than exist today, and under the stabilizing influence of an income maintenance program.

In the final analysis, it is not the case for social justice, or that stability in farm income is needed because of the character of agricultural production or markets, which points to the need for a direct income policy for commercial agriculture. It is the practical recognition that with imperfect knowledge—economic and political—a government would be wise to permit a free market economy to allocate production, determine the output mix, set prices for consumers and farmers in a way which would approximate a system with economic efficiency and only intervene when this system creates cyclical behavior in, and other external diseconomies for, the well-being of specific individuals.

A government could be confident that for commercial farmers as a body in agriculture after the transition period occurs, the free market system (freer than at present) would maximize their joint economic welfare, as it would for consumers, farm suppliers, and all others involved in agriculture. Such a system would maximize economic welfare dynamically; that is, changes in tastes, preferences, production inputs, technology, and so on would be adjusted for naturally as they occur. Such a system would be acceptable since an individual would know that if the economically efficient system does not maximize his own welfare specifically, the government would effect a transfer of wealth as compensation.

WHO THE COMMERCIAL FARMERS WILL BE

In the sense of this discussion, commercial farmers can be most simply defined as those who would remain in agricultural production after a period of transition has passed. Stated differently, they are the farmers for whom adjustment means growth, not out-migration or semiretirement in the sector. This does not include all those who are currently classified as "commercial" by 1966 Census of Agriculture definition (a farmer earning $2,500 or more from sales of agricultural products), since many in this class would leave agriculture during the adjustment process.

Scientific inquiry into the factors influencing the rate of out-migration from and stagnation in agriculture has shown that the farmer's resource base (capital, land), availability of off-farm employment in his region, and his personal characteristics such as education, age, and farm skills are of significance.[2] Changes in technology favoring mechanization and changes in the ratio of input to output prices (profit squeeze) put pressure on smaller farmers to expand or leave farming. But farmers who are already small in terms of low gross income show themselves to be comparatively resource poor; having a poor base to start with, they seem to have little chance of growing and earning incomes in agriculture comparable to nonfarm alternative incomes. Large farmers, faced with the same alternatives (i.e., grow or leave), have the resource base upon which further growth can be built.

One would expect that the participants in agriculture after the transitional period, say in 1981, would be those who are relatively younger and already earning large gross incomes in agriculture in 1971. There is some evidence to suggest that the farm which will be in operation in 1981 (i.e., the commercial farm) will be the one whose current gross income exceeds $10,000 per annum and whose operator is not now over forty-five years old. For example, in a forecast of the number of farms in Ontario in 1981, it was shown that if qualitative trends observed in the postwar period continue, one could expect (1) a decline in the number of farms operated by individuals now older than forty-five, regardless of current gross income position; and (2) a decline (or at best a moderate increase) in the number of farms now operated by farmers between the ages of thirty-five and forty-four (again

2. See B. B. Perkins and D. E. Hathaway, Movement of Labour Between Farm and Non-Farm Jobs, Mich. Agr. Expt. Sta., Res. Bull. 13, 1966.

regardless of current income level).[3] Among younger farmers under thirty-five with current incomes under $10,000, numbers also declined.

If the basic assumptions of this study are accepted as applying to Canada as a whole, which is reasonable, given that Ontario has about 25 percent of Canadian farms and a wide variety of farm types, one might expect the 1971 census to show about 336 thousand commercial farmers (by census definition), but about 124 thousand by our definition. In addition there could be another 36 thousand farmers who, by virtue of their youth and borderline condition, could survive with help. (See Appendix A.)

Again, these quantities are guideposts for a consideration of qualitative policy changes, not as a hard basis upon which quantitative policy should be founded. Yet the typology is useful in showing not only the character of the individuals considered as commercial farmers (Appendix, Table A3) and their number, but also the magnitude of the adjustment of resources which needs to occur. This emphasizes the need for income maintenance and supplementation programs in the decade ahead.

One would expect that the farm sector in 1981 would contain a high proportion of those individuals who are now forty-five years of age and younger and earning gross incomes of at least $10,000 in agriculture. In addition, there will be semiretired and part-time farmers as now, but these will not contribute to output in any large degree. (See Appendix A, Tables A3 and A4.) This represents an agricultural reorganization both in terms of growth for those in the sector and out-migration of many others, which is too large and complex to be planned specifically in all details even if sophisticated quantitative economic models of the sector were available. The alternative is a return to a free market mechanism to effect the structural adjustment while minimizing the costs of the adjustment for specific individuals.

Programs of adjustment for those who are considered to be noncommercial farmers in the context of this

3. R. W. Crown, Forecasting Farm Labour Employment in Ontario to 1981 (M. Sc. thesis; Univ. of Guelph, Guelph, Ontario, 1968), p. 21.

book will be discussed in the following chapter. For those who are currently commercial, an income support scheme to help them adjust to free market operations is given, as is a long-term program of income maintenance.

The question essentially boils down to this: Given the expectation that even with the character of agricultural policy as it now exists and regardless of quantitative policy changes (e.g., changes in the initial prices of wheat and the enlargement of quotas), (1) the Canadian agricultural sector will shrink from about 336 thousand farms in 1971 to about 250 thousand in 1981 with no loss in aggregate output; (2) as part of the overall decline, the poorest farm classes ($250-$4,999 gross sales) can be expected to halve, the young but not-so-poor ($5,000-$10,000 gross sales) fall to 75 percent of their current number, but the older remain virtually locked into low income agriculture; (3) in addition, even the young and relatively well-to-do (in excess of $10,000 gross sales) will decline in importance as the farm operator population tends to become weighted by older operators; (4) this latter tendency portends even greater declines in farm numbers past 1981, because rates of new entry can be expected to decline; and (5) in spite of this the relative importance of those with incomes in excess of $10,000 will grow. Should the public allow those who will leave agriculture to leave and bear the entire cost of that action unaided, while those who remain and grow receive financial support through indirect and commodity subsidies? Or, as an alternative, should the public aid the poor and the out-migration directly and let the free market reflect the quantity and variety of commodities traded and the prices for which they trade?

The following programs assume the latter to be the desirable alternative, with the rider that even those who remain and grow should be helped to minimize the cost of growth and uncertainty.

ELEMENTS OF THE INCOME POLICY FOR COMMERCIAL FARMERS

The basic element of a desirable income policy for commercial farmers is that their income is eventually determined by the value society puts on their products in free markets; that is, their income is determined by the market prices received, quantities sold, and the competitive prices of inputs. This is the concept of agriculture which has served as the ideal, if not the fact, for many years, applied alike to those for whom it was an appropriate way of determining their level of well-being and to those for whom it was inappropriate (smaller scale, noncommercial farmers). This means that a period must elapse during which the current policy mix with the typical price support and quantity manipulation programs (such as those discussed in Part 1) is phased out. Concurrently, some farmers will decide on out-migration, some will retire, and others will base new growth upon all or part of the resources so freed.

In this adjustment period government would assist by ensuring that individuals make their decision based on knowledge of farm and nonfarm conditions, and would act to facilitate the mobility of resources between farms. Government could also act as the interim (or even final) owner of resources in the process of mobility if time lags in reuse were evident. Throughout the adjustment period fluctuations, as well as permanent declines, in realized incomes would occur in anticipation of which a program of direct income support would be required for commercial and noncommercial farmers. Other complementary programs would be required to insure that interim adjustment proceeded as smoothly as possible, notably in the areas concerning inputs into production (land, labor, capital, and management) and supply management. In such complementary policies government would essentially be removing constraints to adjustment.[4] These two topics are considered separately below.

Eventually, perhaps in a decade, one could anticipate that many of the programs required in the adjust-

---

4. See Darrel H. Plaunt, Implications of the Outlook for Adjustment, a paper presented to the Canadian Agricultural Outlook Conference, Ottawa, Nov. 1969. In his paper Plaunt convincingly defines the need for policies to aid adjustment as the need to remove constraints on mobility, and mitigate the effects of variables essentially out of governments' control, such as market demand.

ment period could be terminated, particularly direct income support to many individuals migrating out who would be absorbed into nonfarm occupations. At this time the policy for commercial farmers would switch from emphasizing income support to emphasizing income maintenance and stability. Again, complementing programs of resource use and supply management would be necessary to insure that income maintenance programs continue to work. (See Chap. 7 and 8.) For if the unhampered market is to determine, to a large degree, the volume and distribution of income in the postadjustment agricultural sector, government could minimize its outlays on income stabilizing and maintenance programs by continuing to invest moderate sums in market analysis and control, technological change, or information diffusion.

PROGRAMS IMPLEMENTING THE INCOME POLICY

Because of the insurmountable difficulty involved in a governmental agency's defining a program with enough subdefinitions and qualifications to meet all individual families' particular circumstances and ambitions, the program to implement the income policy for commercial farmers would require that a degree of choice be left to persons now engaged in agriculture.

Even though "commercial" farmers have been defined in this chapter as those who at the 1971 census would be less than forty-five years old and earning $10,000 in gross revenue from farming operations (with no significant nonfarm work), there are undoubtedly individuals, older and younger, with gross sales receipts between $5,000 and $10,000, who could organize good, viable farm operations and be fully in agricultural employment in 1981.

Thus, in the following income support and maintenance programs for commercial farmers, individuals should be permitted to declare whether they wish to be viewed as potentially commercial farmers and participate as such until circumstances force them to consider out-migration (if ever). Nonetheless, in making the choice to be considered commercial farmers, they would be obliged to "play the game" by the rules defined for commercial farmers in the stricter sense just given and not expect special conciliatory treatment. They would, on the other hand, be permitted, and indeed encouraged, to grow by using programs available and specified for the purpose of removing the constraints to in-sectoral adjustment (Chap. 7 and 8). Alternately once it became evident during the transition period that a farmer had erred in his decision to be viewed as a commercial farmer, the individual should be allowed to opt for inclusion in the plans described for noncommercial farmers.

However, certain economic realities of the situation must be recognized. Hence, the plan to be described as obtaining for commercial farmers would not be open to farmers who in census year 1971 had cash receipts of $5,000 or less. Farmers in this income class have a high probability of earning less than $2,500 net income from farming operations, and only exceed defined poverty level incomes by having upwards of thirty-three days of off-farm employment.[5] (A poverty level income is defined by the Task Force as being below $3,000 per annum, with the indication that this value is based on 1967 data and the suggestion that it be raised in any new calculation.) Further, of about 200 thousand farmers with less than $5,000 in gross receipts, only 67 thousand had enough off-farm employment to be above the poverty level. When an alternative plan is available, specifically designed for persons whose only real hope for attaining an income above poverty is in out-migration from agriculture to retirement, it would be holding out false hope to even suggest that a farm whose earning capacity is below $5,000 might become commercial by permitting these farmers to participate in the commercial farm income policy.

With these general comments in mind, an operational description of the programs involved could be as follows:

Program 1: Transitional Income Support

Purpose. To compensate commercial farmers for net income lost during the period in which agriculture ad-

5. Federal Task Force on Agriculture, Canadian Agriculture in the Seventies (Ottawa: Queen's Printer, 1970), p. 418 ff.

justs to the market-determined sets of prices, reflected demands, scale economies, market-determined input costs, and so on, which would follow after subsidies and other price-commodity manipulation programs are cancelled.

Eligibility. All farmers (defined by census as full-time farmers) would be eligible for this program, even if initially their net farm income is below $5,000, without regard to commodities produced or location. Only the portion of income earned in farming would be considered to be "supportable," and only farm families in agriculture as of the census date would be allowed to participate. This condition assures that future new farmers' entry into agriculture is based on the true need of society for them, reflected through free markets, not a false need artificially created by supported prices.

Transferability and Capitalization of Program Value. Income supplements would be tied to the farm family and hence would not be transferable with resources. This means that the program would not have a stable or negotiable "present value" and could not become capitalized into the value of fixed farm resources; this is in contrast to current commodity-based programs which do add to fixed asset value.

Families who leave agriculture (out-migrants) could be permitted to claim the supplement for a few years after departure if this is deemed desirable as an incentive to their leaving. This would ease their departure in that it would supplement their income over and above that to which they are entitled as an out-migrant if they qualify (see Chap. 6). Finally, capitalization of this program into fixed asset value would be frustrated, since the program would terminate after the period of adjustment.

Time Period. Income supplementation would proceed under "full supplementation" provisions for about five years after the date of implementation. After this time the rate of supplementation would be decreased annually until the 1981 program of income maintenance is introduced.

This timing would be sufficient for a currently commercial farmer to attain significant adjustment in his operations, particularly with the kinds of complementary program envisaged (Chap. 7 and 8). Further, it would permit the farmer who opts for this plan, but is not really expected to be successful, to see if his choice was a right choice, while leaving him income support if he later decides to leave.

Terms and Conditions. Individuals wishing to participate in the program would be required to show a true account of their gross and net incomes before and after the start of the program. Income tax statements could be considered best for this purpose, since they would show the real net revenue of the farm (returns to owner and family labor, owned land and capital, and management). This source would be consistent with the best source of income data used in the posttransition period income stabilization program (Program 3). This would establish the degree to which an individual would lose net revenue because of adjustment, and thus has a right to compensation and an appropriate percentage of net farm income to be granted as a bonus. This would be the individual's base for support for the next five years.

Although extensive analysis of farm accounts or other sources would be required to compute the appropriate tables to be used in compensation, the following situation might prevail:

1. Some evidence suggests that for low income farms ($5,000-$7,499 gross sales) net revenue is approximately 45 percent of gross revenue.[6] The average net revenue for all farms in all income classes in 1966 was 40 percent of realized gross income.[7] This suggests that as farm gross incomes enlarge, the ratio of net to gross income declines. This is supported by the theoretical contention that as a farm grows, it first realizes increased and then de-

6. Federal Task Force, Canadian Agriculture in the Seventies, p. 420.

7. See W. L. Porteous, Canadian Farm Income Levels and Distribution, paper presented to Canadian Agricultural Outlook Conference, Ottawa, Nov. 1969, p. 4.

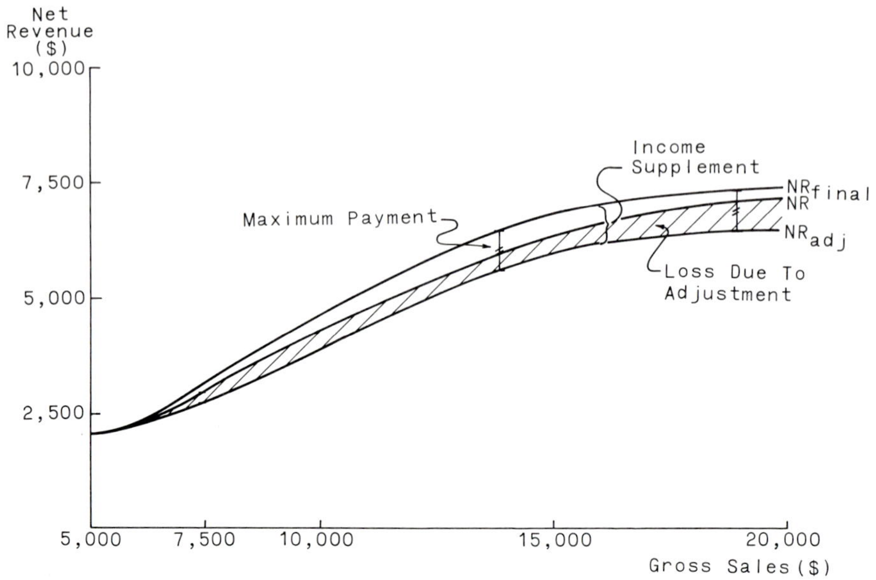

FIG. 5.1. Net revenue, adjusted net revenue, and income subsidy by dollar value of gross sales.

creasing returns to added resources. This gives the curve NR in Figure 5.1.

2. It was shown in Chapter 2 that typical support mechanisms in agriculture favor large farms over smaller farms. If, on an average, federal and provincial governments in Canada provide assistance amounting to about 9 percent[8] of current gross realized farm income, or about $1,100 per farm, large farms probably gain more from this, but small farms less, since programs tend to be commodity- or input-based and small farms produce and use less. Thus, if all current supportive programs were eliminated to spur adjustment, farms could lose different absolute amounts of net income. However, the loss would not really be $1,100 per farm even on an average, since about 48 percent of this support would be contained in programs not cancelled: it

8. S. W. Garland and S. C. Hudson, Government Involvement in Agriculture, a report to the Federal Task Force on Agriculture (Ottawa: Queen's Printer, 1970).

represents programs that do not actually transfer funds to the farm sector.[9] Under the scheme proposed, some of these activities would be retained as programs to assist adjustment. Therefore, NR_{adj} in Figure 5.1 represents the likely net revenue position of farmers during adjustment and is below NR by about 4.5 percent of the gross revenue involved.

3. Compensation would be made for the loss of income due to adjustment. This would close the gap between NR and NR_{adj} in Figure 5.1. In addition, to secure public support, a bonus could be paid (a constant percentage amount—e.g., 50 percent of gross income) to all participants.
4. To prevent abuses of the program and to limit the demands of individuals for payments, no single farm family would be compensated in excess of $1,500 per year for the first five years. This principle of limiting the absolute dollar value of support per farm has already been accepted (but not without dissent) in the United States. Under these conditions the income supplements would not alter the marginal costs or revenues of units produced in the future, and would not directly encourage production (as do the current indirect and direct subsidies which relate to per unit quantities of commodities transported or produced). These terms could easily be varied to account for regional differences or particular farms considered to be adversely affected by adjustment in special situations. But for continued adjustment, significant deviation from or differentiation of the standard scheme should be avoided.

After the initial five-year period, the complete program would be phased out over another five-year period, perhaps with a 20 percent annual reduction in benefits paid "across the board."

Implementation. A public educational program could be organized to explain to both farm and urban people (1) the reasons why farming has income problems as a result of technological revaluation, economic develop-

9. Garland and Hudson, Government Involvement, table 93.

ment, inelastic demand, and educational and geographic separation from economic opportunity in urban centers, and (2) the societal advantages of the proposed system over commodity programs, indirect subsidies, and existing supply control programs through quotas. Emphasis would be placed on explaining that (1) commodity and input subsidies, direct and indirect, are inefficient means of attaining desired income levels for farmers relative to direct income supplementation, and (2) supply control, which could obtain a given increment of income for the farm sector, is actually paid for indirectly by all consumers of the food item through the market. Income is transferred in a manner retrogressive to the income of consumers, and is an unending transfer. On the other hand, the same income increment coming as direct payments from the treasury would be progressive in its taxing effect on consumers and based on recognizable value-earned principles.

Administration. Existing personnel in the Canadian Department of Agriculture, freed from duties surrounding the administration of price support schemes, could administer the proposed program with complete impartiality. Officials of ARDA would probably have the advantage in administering the programs in Chapter 6 and some of the complementary programs of Chapter 7, since those activities most closely parallel their existing programs.

Costs. Conceivably in the initial year of the program there would be about 68 thousand farms with sales volumes in excess of $15,000 and an additional 56 thousand farms with sales volumes in the $10,000-$15,000 range (Appendix A). Of the farm operators with sales volumes between $5,000 and $9,999, who might consider themselves "commercial" and seek growth, presumably only those younger than forty-five years of age could remain and grow. Hence, there would be an additional 36 thousand potential commercial farmers in 1971.

Even if every commercial farmer in 1971 claimed the maximum annual benefit under Program 1, the total budget for the program would be about $240 million (Table 5.1). If, as would be more likely, the farmers in low-

Table 5.1. Costs of Program 1, Compared with 1966-67 Federal-Provincial Joint Expenditures

	Year of Program 1	2	3	4	5	6	7	8	9	10	Decade Total
Program 1											
(i) Maximum per farm benefit[a] ($)	1,500	1,500	1,500	1,500	1,500	1,200	900	600	300	0	...
(ii) Farms receiving benefit[b] (000s)	160	160	160	160	160	160	160	160	160	160	...
(iii) Cost (i) × (ii) ($ million)	240	240	240	240	240	192	144	96	48	0	1,640
Current programs											
(iv) Annual cost[c] ($ million)	442	442	442	442	442	442	442	442	442	442	4,420
(v) Saving by eliminating only production and price supports[c] ($ million)	317	317	317	317	317	317	317	317	317	317	3,170
(vi) Net cost of current programs retained (iv)-(v) ($ million)	125	125	125	125	125	125	125	125	125	125	1,250
New program cost											
(vii) With program 1 included (vi) + (iii) ($ million)	365	365	365	365	365	317	269	221	173	125	2,930
(viii) Annual saving over present (iv) − (vii) ($ million)	77	77	77	77	77	125	173	221	269	317	1,490

Note: Figures in this table have been estimated based on assumptions in text.
[a]See "Terms and Conditions" in text.
[b]See "Costs" in text.
[c]See Table 1.1.

er income classes claimed less (a farmer with a gross income of $10,000 would have to show loss of net income of about 20 percent resulting from cancellation of the indirect programs), the total cost would be less.

Considering the life of the program, that is, five years at full benefits and five years at gradually reduced benefits, and assuming no net change in the number of farms affected (although in fact one would expect a net decline in the number of farms even in the large farm classes over the decade (see Appendix A, Table A4) the ten-year cost of the program would be about $1.64 billion.

How do these costs compare with the costs of programs already in effect? In Table 1.1 combined federal and provincial expenditures on agriculture in 1966-67 showed the following allotments: $137 million (31 percent)—production assistance, $20 million (4.5 percent) marketing assistance; $180 million (40.5 percent)—price supports and income assistance; $21 million (4.5 percent)—extension; $59 million (13.5 percent)—research; $9 million (2 percent)—education; and $16 million (4 percent)—administration; total—$442 million. If only those programs which were involved with production assistance, price supports, and income assistance were superseded by Program 1, the government could achieve the same ends at a saving of at least $77 million annually (Table 5.1). No new staff would be required if existing staff assignments were reallocated, and no other program would have to be foregone. Over the decade, in the unlikely event that the cost of existing government programs do not rise (which they would if only because they both stimulate production and try to maintain prices simultaneously) the implementation of Program 1 could lead to a saving of $1.5 billion. This is illustrated in Table 5.1. With $1.5 billion, government could simply give $9,000 to each farm operator who in 1971 would be expected to leave serious agriculture by 1981 (about 166 thousand under the new programs).

Program 2: Income Stabilization and Maintenance for Commercial Agriculture

Purposes. The ten-year period of direct income support would provide compensation to farmers for income depression resulting from structural transformation and any short-run growth in supply capacity. In this period farm incomes would be protected at equitable levels while increasingly being determined by market forces. At the end of the transition period, direct income supplementation would be completely phased out, allowing farm income to be determined solely by market interactions. To prevent a recurrence of the unfavorable farm income situation which Program 1 sought to remedy, a program aimed at income stability (rather than price stability) would be phased in.

Eligibility. Any census farmer would be eligible.

Transferability. None (as in Program 1).

Time Period. Perpetual.

Terms and Conditions. Among the many alternates, two are discussed here:

1. The program to provide income stability could work as follows: The average income over a few years of each farmer before income support payments were made (as substantiated by his income tax returns) would serve as his income base. He would then be guaranteed an income equal to a fraction of this base.

   The base is essentially a moving average: it would increase for farmers expanding operations, while declining for those phasing down. Should there be a long-run downward trend in farm prices, farmers who maintain a static operation would have a declining income base. At this signal, the individual would opt for the low income program if he desired. Those who expand, take advantage of new technology, or develop other efficiencies to offset the price decline would maintain the same base if the forces offset each other, or would have an increasing base if farming advances more than offset the price decline. Income losses through contingencies such as drought, hail, early frost, or unusual and stochastic price breaks would be compensated automatically under this income stability program. No other scheme would be necessary for this purpose. Finally, each farmer could be given a minimum, below which his income would not be allowed to fall.

2. Among currently discussed and other prospective programs to achieve the stated objective are negative income tax schemes, which permit an individual to claim a credit for income from the treasury if his realized income in a current year falls below some prescribed minimum level, or a level representing the individual's historic real income.[10] These proposals would serve the farm sector with efficiency similar to the nonfarm sector if the income level called the "break-even income" (i.e., the income at which no tax is paid, below which a supplement is given, and above which taxes are paid in the normal way) is high enough to be sensitive to the changes in price, production, weather, tastes, and so on that create instability in farm incomes. To illustrate, if the break-even annual income were universally set at $3,000 (net realized income) and an individual's usual annual income was, say, $5,000, his income could fluctuate downward by $2,000 in any given year before he would gain from the program. This break-even income condition would render the program useless. On the other hand, if they had been realizing an average of $4,500 for the past five years, then an income in the next year of $4,000 (a fluctuation of $500 from his base) would be enough to permit him to gain from the program. We should remember that we are not discussing "poor" people in this proposal, but commercial farmers.

---

10. An excellent and brief exposition of several alternate schemes is Southern Extension Public Affairs Committee, Family Income Maintenance: Some Options (Washington: Ext. Serv., USDA, May 1970).

Finally, one could devise a feature whereby income in excess of the individual's base or break-even income is subject to a tax surcharge, as if it were a de facto capital gain, or windfall. But this feature would not really be politically acceptable.

Implementation and Administration. At this time it is difficult to predict who would administer the income stability program. Certainly those in the Canadian Department of Agriculture who have worked with the income support program of the preceding decade would be influential. Even if the scheme were were broader, encompassing both farm and nonfarm families, the Department of Agriculture would have a role to play, particularly in insuring that the program achieve goals of stability for commercial agriculture.

Costs. Apart from the administration of this program, which could be done at virtually no net cost if the personnel previously employed in cancelled programs were used, costs under this program would be primarily in the form of foregone government revenue with a minimal government outlay.

However, the feature providing a surcharge on income in excess of the base income would mean that the program would run at zero net cost over a period of time, since one might expect that extra government revenues and foregone revenues would even out if both resulted from truly random exogenous shocks in the economy at large.

Program 3: Restructuring and Reorienting Commodity-Oriented Programs

Purpose. With Programs 1 and 2 implemented to support income in a period of transition for agriculture, the need for policies aimed at raising prices through commodity-withholding actions, paying subsidies for output, and subsidizing inputs would have vanished, except for a few specific instances considered in Chapters 7 and 8. Since many of the existing agricultural programs have counter-adjustment forces, their continued existence would tend to frustrate the adjustment-facilitating programs described in Programs 1 and 2. Program 3 is essentially a program to encourage, enforce, and otherwise restructure specific commodity-oriented programs that have evolved over Canada's agricultural history, away from practices which hamper natural adjustment of agriculture under market forces, to those which help accelerate adjustment or at least permit it to take place. As such it does not have specific terms and timing (although it has priorities) but is rather a set of guidelines for change. It could be considered a program of housecleaning.

Elements

1. There are in Canada 120 provincial marketing boards whose functions vary over a range of activities from managing and restricting output flows, operating teletype market networks for produce, managing two-price systems, and conducting promotional campaigns, alone and in combination. Some of these activities are oriented toward improving the demand outlook and conditions for the product involved. The vast majority of the effort, however, is directed toward supply restriction.[11] One cannot generally find fault with the activities of such boards as they apply to demand-increasing activities although these may simply be a waste of producers' money. One cannot hope to expand demand for a particular commodity to the extent required to absorb the productive capacity of producers' enterprises, or realize gains without conflict with near-substitutes. Nor can one generally find fault with efforts to organize markets to stimulate competition among buyers. A good example of this activity is the teletype marketing system for hogs in Ontario.

   But legislation to remove the power of marketing boards from supply-restricting activity should be considered, particularly in the administration of quota systems involved and in the case of so many products where storage rationing or market queuing is not a problem (as it is in grain). Alternate means of supply control which do not require quotas

---

11. Federal Task Force, <u>Canadian Agriculture in the Seventies</u>, Chap. 12, p. 311.

(and so are not counter-adjustment) are given in Chapter 8.

2. A large number of specific government programs aimed at providing subsidies for management inputs, transportation, commodity prices, and so on, have been instituted. All these activities have been more or less directed toward reducing the cost of production of some commodities, or paying a commodity price which exceeds normal market expectation. Some have been referred to as "income support" measures, but as has been explained in Chapter 2 the effect has been to widen the income gap between farm and nonfarm incomes and increase the disparity between rich and poor farmers. Approximately 40 percent of Canadian government expenditures on agriculture have been for these programs. (See Table 1.1.) About 85 percent of these are federal government expenditures.

A second broad category of government programs which would continue to have harmful effects on adjustment in the transition period is the production assistance programs category, accounting for about 31 percent of total expenditures. Half of these expenditures are made by provincial governments with equal amounts being added by the federal government. It is in these two categories that the great paradox of Canadian agricultural policy is seen: 40 percent of the expenditures are required to support the prices and incomes which 31 percent of the expenditures help to deteriorate (because of already large and excess capacity in production and inelastic final demands for food). Indirect production assistance as it relates to some inputs is of value (such as the research, education, and extension services) and should be part of any new alignment of government expenditure on agriculture. But these account for only 20 percent of government expenditures. The production assistance rendered in bringing new land under cultivation (as opposed to consolidating land already under cultivation) or granting subsidies on credit (based on some mistaken beliefs which are discussed in Chapter 7), and so on, tends merely to aggravate trends in the rate at which structural transformation occurs and output potential grows in agriculture and should be abandoned.

The third broad category of governmental expenditure which can be questioned is the 4.5 percent spent on marketing assistance of commodities. To the extent that these funds subsidize transportation rates and otherwise try to allocate "market shares" among farmers who would not otherwise be efficient enough to compete, this class of expenditure retards adjustment interregionally and within agriculture and slows the rate of withdrawal among those who could be better served by programs outlined in Chapter 6. However, to the extent that this marketing assistance is promotional in nature and directed toward creating competition between buyers, the results are beneficial for adjustment. Yet even here the producer should consider this type of expenditure as a firm's cost of production, and not expect government subsidy. This is not to say that a producer marketing board could not perform the function at members' expense. The point is that if such expenditures are worth undertaking from a benefits-to-cost analysis viewpoint, then the direct beneficiary should pay the cost directly. Governments could safely eliminate programs such as those described above when programs like 1 and 2 are instituted; and if adjustment of agriculture to a self-sufficient status for commercial farmers is the goal, these expenditures should cease.

If the goal behind the programs recommended for cancellation is to provide welfare transfers for agriculture, even then there are less expensive means of doing the job (Chap. 6).

Timing. This program would call for a phased cancellation of the expenditures designated above, over perhaps two to three years, beginning with the withdrawal of major price supports immediately.

Implementation. Legislation would be required to rescind the powers of provincial marketing boards over quota control. This could be done by declaring them no longer compulsory, or by having them actually agree to give up the quota administration power in exchange for the power to administer positive or negative supply management as described in Chapter 8.

Administrative procedures could be used to accomplish most other restructuring.

A federal-provincial conference on agricultural policy could coordinate the changeover in policy direction.

Costs. No financial cost is required for this program; it is, in essence, a process of saving. The psychological and political costs of the program could be minimal if the program were implemented in a phased manner and with appropriate preconditioning of farmers and consumers, and if it were made clear that no jobs would be lost because of the program, and no nongovernment organization would be forced to disband. Indeed, far from being a challenge to the survival of institutions as they now exist, Program 3 is a challenge to their flexibility and would allow them to serve the public in effective ways. Some alternative roles for these institutions are discussed in subsequent chapters.

CONCLUSION

The programs suggested here would mark a clear break with the Canadian agricultural policy tradition with respect to government support of commercial agriculture. There would be a swing away from the input and output subsidization schemes of the past which, as previously shown, create problems for commercial as well as noncommercial farmers.

Two short-term programs would combine to rid the nation of the preponderance of micro-level programs which have accumulated over the past twenty-five years; and a program of direct compensation would redress the ill effects of restructuring as they are felt by individuals. Eventually these short-run programs themselves would be phased out as their useful lives end. After the transition period a fully rationalized and market-guided agricultural sector would operate under the protection of a system of direct income maintenance devised as insurance against the vagaries of weather, fluctuating foreign trade, distinct technical changes, and the other instabilities of commodity cycles in production and markets.

In the process, the cost of government involvement in commercial agriculture as a supporter of income would decrease, making the agricultural industry more like other industries in the general economy, with recognition of some of the unique problems of agricultural production and commodities already mentioned.

6 An Income Policy for Noncommercial or Low Income Farmers

A MOST SIGNIFICANT realization of recent years sees agriculture as having within it a class of farms destined to be chronically poor, and agricultural policy to date as having done nothing to alleviate the misery of those people involved. With low levels of output, these farm families participate only minimally in organized markets, and hence do not derive significant absolute amounts of income or benefit from price support or stabilization programs. Relying largely on farm-originated inputs, they derive no benefit from subsidies on inputs and transportation services. Being resource poor, they derive no benefit from management counseling, research results, or extension services. No recombination of their resources, no matter how specialized, for the production of given outputs would yield enough revenue to provide them with an improved standard of living.

Thus with reorganization, subsidization, and added knowledge about farming recognized as being generally ineffective as solutions to the income problem of poor farmers, some other programs have been proposed. Several solutions have been suggested: some are built on the belief that time will solve the problem if agriculture is left alone; some are founded on the belief that rural industrialization will help; but most claim that if small farms grew (that is, if they enlarged their resource base) they could more fully participate in the market and earn larger incomes which the market would provide. Indeed, if a few individuals followed the prescription they would undoubtedly benefit to some degree. This is the essence of the view that some farmers under forty-five, and in the $5,000-

$9,999 income class could in fact become commercial farmers, although it must be recognized that even doubling some farms' resources and doubling net income would leave the farm family in poverty.

For consolidation of resources alone to be successful in raising income for a large number of farmers, (1) many other farmers would have to give up their claims to some resources (notably land), and (2) the farms newly employing the resources would have to have scale economies which make the resources less productive in new use than they were in the former use. If either of these conditions does not hold, income conditions will worsen in that (1) excess demand for resources would tend to raise actual or imputed input prices and tend to depress income, and (2) product prices would experience more downward pressure, since more output would be produced with the resources in the new use than was lost by the resources moving out of the vanishing farm. Hence growth in farm resource employment alone cannot solve the problems of poverty in agriculture, whether the acquisition of resources is subsidized or not.

Yet it is in this spirit, with the goal of growth stimulation in mind, that many current programs aimed at "adjustment" are conducted. Much less attention has been paid to what Plaunt has called "adjustment out of agriculture,"[1] although this tendency may be changing. In at least one province, the director of the Agricultural and Rural Development Association (ARDA) has indicated that

> The key word to ARDA programming in the 70's is ADJUSTMENT
>
> —adjustment of both low and medium range income farmers into viable operations
>
> —adjustment of low income farmers and agriculture into either non-farm employment, farm employment or into retirement

---

1. Darrel H. Plaunt, Implications of the Outlook for Adjustment, paper presented to the Canadian Agricultural Outlook Conference, Ottawa, Nov. 1969.

—adjustment of low income rural people into nonfarm employment.[2]

Thus with a more accurate definition of what is really meant by a "commercial" or "viable" farm (such as that used in the preceding chapter), and by implication, what is really meant by a noncommercial, nonviable, low income farm sector, it is easily concluded that the need is not for programs to facilitate growth and in-sector adjustment, but rather programs to minimize the hardships of withdrawal on farm families. The essential character of an income policy for noncommercial farmers should be that the solution of their personal low income problems will be found either by their finding employment in the nonfarm sector, or their receiving outright government transfers while they continue in semiretirement in the farm sector. To date, a class of programs has been instituted in Canada not specifically designed for farmers but from which it is hoped that all rural poor, including poverty-level farmers, will derive income benefits. These programs, the Fund for Regional Economic Development (FRED) and the Area Development Agency (ADA), are administered by the federal Department of Regional Economic Expansion (DREE). They have attempted to develop industrial, educational, and service structures within specified regions, through subsidization of firms, grants, loans, and so on.

There are several economic questions that might be raised about this kind of development assistance in general; for example, whether government transfers should be used to alter the comparative advantage of competing regions when the private sector has not placed a high enough value on the development to undertake it on its own. Yet there would, no doubt, be clear cases in which government sponsorship of infrastructural inputs into a region could be sufficient to spur further development by the private sector. On the

2. H. F. Crown, The ARDA Program in Ontario: A Position Statement and Outlook, notes for discussion with the ARDA branch field staff at their conference, Nov. 1969, Barrie, Ontario.

other hand experience in the United States where this kind of program has been attempted is instructive. For example, considerable infrastructural investment has been made by the U.S. Government in the Appalachian region of the United States, but comparatively little has been undertaken in, say Iowa. Yet the industrialization of Iowa has proceeded at a considerably faster rate than Appalachia's.

Industrialization, or at least nonfarm job opportunities, tend to appear where agriculture is itself strong and viable. This lesson of experience is consistent with what has come to be regarded as the "correct" normative view of economic development when applied to developing nations. The approach to economic development offered in the 1950s could be characterized as forcing rapid industrialization in hopes that the new activity so generated would force the growth and development of "supplier sectors." The reasoning was essentially valid as far as it went. But an underlying assumption seemed to be that supplier sectors could be found within the nation undergoing industrialization, with the result that industrialization would spread the benefits of increased income back through the country. The belief was in serious error, for the development of advanced industrial sectors generally created demands not for supplies that could be offered by the country itself at competitive costs, but by sectors in countries already developed, usually the advanced western nations. The new industrial sectors therefore developed stronger trade links with similar sectors in other countries than with the primary producing sectors in their own nation. The growing wealth of the industrial sectors tended to be retained in those sectors rather than dispersed, so that domestic disparities of income worsened.

An analogous situation could be envisaged between the various regions of Canada as a result of the use of forced development in poorer regions. It is possible that if an industrial firm were located in a rural region with the help of a subsidy (with tax relief, government-provided site, etc.) that the majority of the labor employed would be imported into the region along with the plant. Rural persons with the personal characteristics, educational backgrounds, and aspirations that would open nonfarm employment to them as an alternative to farming could reasonably be expected to have already left farming,[3] and the remaining potential labor force would tend to be less desirable than labor relocated from towns. Certainly there would be some infusion of money into the poor region as a result of the industrial workers' purchases of personal items, but this would probably be a small fraction of the total spending generated by the plant. This spending for goods and services would benefit town business, but it would be of little relevance to poor and noncommercial farmers.

The currently more acceptable approach in prescribing economic development of nations seems to be that one should exploit the sectors in which the comparative advantage is found, and develop through a set of linkages with suppliers and customers until a strong economic fiber is woven. But even this holds no direct hope for the economically disadvantaged, although it could supply an environment in which potential outmigrants from agriculture might adjust more easily. (Chapter 7 contains a discussion of programs which could help Canadian agriculture adjust more smoothly, and at less cost to government and individuals than at present.)

Lastly, it is just not reasonable from the standpoint of social justice to hope that given enough time the low income problem in agriculture might solve itself. Age distribution and low prospects for mobility among low income farmers suggest that natural processes would take too long and would involve too high a financial cost for the individuals involved.[4]

---

3. Evidence for this is seen in the general discussion in Jane A. Abramson, Barriers to Population Mobility: Four Economically Lagging Areas in the Atlantic Provinces and Quebec (Ottawa: Canadian Center for Community Studies, 1968); or C. E. Bishop, Economic Aspects of Migration from Farms in the United States, in Labor Mobility and Population in Agriculture (Ames: Iowa State Univ. Press, 1961).

4. This conclusion is supported by the Federal Task Force on Agriculture, Canadian Agriculture in the Seventies (Ottawa: Queen's Printer, 1970), p. 410.

The estimates of the rate of decline in the number of farms of different economic classes operated by farmers of different ages (Appendix A, Table A4) show that although a rapid out-migration could be expected among the young, many would remain in agriculture at poverty levels without a specific program to help them. Thus with the passage of time, industrialization of rural regions, or adjustment within agriculture essentially ruled out as reasonable alternatives in the attack on low incomes of noncommercial farmers, direct government action through specifically pointed programs seems to be the answer. This is not to say that elements of the previous solutions should not be retained in the new programs. But they should be incorporated into programs with a distinctively new flavor which see poverty as it is and attempt to solve the problem directly. Such programs are outlined below.

WHO THE NONCOMMERCIAL FARMERS WILL BE

It would be simple to say that noncommercial farmers are all those who in 1971 are not considered to be commercial farmers by the definition given in Chapter 5—predominantly farmers older than forty-five years of age or with gross incomes of less than $10,000. But this does not generally describe them well. For as we have concluded elsewhere farmers in the low income group are not homogeneous with respect to their ages, aspirations, or owned resources (Appendix A, Table A3).

Within the group are the very poor (those earning no more than $3,000 net income per year from farming operations combined with upwards of thirty-three days of nonfarm labor). These are typically farmers of any age with gross sales per farm of less than $5,000 annually. In 1966 there were about 237 thousand such farmers, operating 55 percent of all Canadian census farms. On a provincial basis the largest proportions of such farms (as a percent of total farms in the province) were found in the Maritimes (77 percent over all). But in absolute number, Ontario had three times the number of poverty-level farms found in the Maritime Provinces combined (58 thousand as opposed to 19 thousand, or about 25 percent of all Canadian poverty-level farms). In 1971 there could reasonably be upwards of 116 thousand such farms (Appendix A, Table A1). The age distribution of this class is strongly skewed toward the over-forty-five category, if Ontario can be considered as representative of the nation as a whole. For Ontario a study indicated that in 1971 one could expect to find about 80 percent of the operators of poverty-level farms over forty-five years of age.[5]

In addition to the very poor, there is a class of farmers who experience low if not poverty-level incomes. In 1966 about 97 thousand farms had annual gross sales receipts of between $5,000 and $10,000. The expected decrease in this class resulting from basic economic motivation would not be large (96 thousand farms in 1971) since they are generally older (62.5 percent over forty-five) and less mobile in terms both of their own growth and of out-migration (see Appendix A, Table A3).

These farmers are not necessarily "resource poor" in the sense that they own nothing; for example, the average dollar value of owned assets among farms with gross sales of $5,000-$7,499 in 1966 was about $43,000. This class of farms, 20 percent of the total 1966 farm number, contributed only 13 percent of the value of products sold. By comparison, the Census of Agriculture, 1966, indicates that farms in the $10,000-$15,000 sales class, which accounted for 15 percent of the farms and 19 percent of the value of output, held an average of about $69,000 of assets in 1966. The problem is that, given the returns to agricultural resources, a capital stock of $43,000 is insufficient to generate a reasonable flow of income for the farm family by nonfarm (or even farm) standards. Therefore the low income farm classes are faced with different problems that require different future action than are the higher income farmers.

There now could be 147 thousand farm operators who by virtue of their age (over forty-five), current income (under $10,000 gross income annually), and as-

5. R. W. Crown, Forecasting Farm Labour Employment in Ontario to 1981 (M. Sc. thesis, Univ. of Guelph, Guelph, Ontario, 1968) table 2.2.

set position might easily be best served by remaining in agriculture in a quasi-retired state with government funds supplementing their incomes. But also there could be 28 thousand farm operators who could migrate from the sector if they so chose and if nonfarm economic activity were sufficient to absorb them.

What is required in both cases is a set of programs which remove the barriers that inhibit the individual from making the appropriate choice. The need is to determine what the unique barriers are in each case and develop programs for their specific removal.

ELEMENTS OF THE INCOME POLICY FOR NONCOMMERCIAL FARMERS

Because there is a wide diversity in the characteristics of noncommercial farmers (Appendix A), several programs seem to be required to alleviate their problems. But in spite of their diversity the common characteristic of the farm poor is that they are now in rural communities and on poor farms, but will probably not be by 1981. This suggests the fundamental element that could serve as a basis for a common policy and program for them.

Most noncommercial farms will tend to disappear within the decade of the seventies, particularly those owned by persons under forty-five years of age (Appendix A, Table A4). But even noncommercial farmers have physical assets which they have accumulated through their efforts. The prospects of losing much of the value of these assets if they were sold can be considered a barrier to liquidation, and hence adjustment. Similarly, the age of most of the noncommercial farmers would tend to limit their usefulness in the nonfarm sector, with the result that they could not expect to be as well off after leaving agriculture as they would be by remaining even at low incomes. This could account for the lower attrition rate among older farmers than younger, and is a second large barrier to the adjustment of older farmers.

Yet these farmers, with human and nonhuman assets (but assets too few to allow them to remain in commercial agriculture) should not be made to bear all the financial costs which adjustment out of agriculture would force upon them. A government policy to assist these farmers to liquidate their assets and recover much of the accumulated value of their farms would ease their adjustment, and would in effect remove even the slight barriers to adjustment that impinge on the majority of them. As a form of financial assistance for the adjustment of noncommercial farmers, policy could be directed toward helping individuals convert their accumulated nonhuman capital (machinery, land, buildings, and livestock) into a steady flow of income which could be spent at the farmer's discretion. This would be, in essence, a capital recovery policy for noncommercial farmers.

Once protected by a capital recovery program against loss of a lifetime's investment if withdrawal were undertaken, some noncommercial farmers would require assistance in actually leaving the sector. These would typically be the younger, better-educated (or retrainable) individuals in the class. Hence, the underlying government effort to facilitate withdrawal of noncommercial farmers from agriculture by guaranteeing them the value of their previous investments could be supplemented by a set of mobility-increasing programs for those who choose out-migration. But for those who, by their own wisdom or through counseling, choose not to migrate, the underlying capital recovery program could be supplemented with lifetime on-farm residency-and-use provisions and direct income supplementation.

One real benefit derived from government sponsoring a program of liquidating the capital on poor and noncommercial farms and thus creating a usable income flow is the secondary income flow this would in turn provide for declining rural communities. A rural community, like any community, must have time to adjust to trends in population, even if this trend is toward extinction. Communities survive on income flows, the re-spending of money in trade, not on the accumulation of inert capital stocks. Under a capital liquidation or recovery program, government would effectively give communities an opportunity to benefit from the capital accumulated on farms in their trading area as well as give them time to adjust to foreseeable future conditions. (More will be said about community assistance in Chapter 7.)

The other real advantage of capital liquidation and supplemental programs is that they work toward a final solution of the rural low income problem by insuring that resources currently on low income farms do not continue to be there generation after generation. If capital is to be passed on from parents to children, when the suggested program is in effect it will be in the form of money wealth, not real estate, machines, or other fixed assets. Thus the poverty cycle could be broken.

PROGRAMS TO IMPLEMENT THE POLICY

In implementing programs for farmers considered to be noncommercial (on the brink of withdrawal from significant agricultural activity), government should guarantee that an individual can express his own aspirations (after counseling, if possible) by permitting him to make a choice among the programs provided. As in the program framework outlined in Chapter 5 in which individuals in the $5,000-$10,000 gross sales class were allowed to opt for the program leading to commercial status or for one leading to withdrawal, so also in this framework would individuals be permitted to decide upon out-migration or de facto retirement while continuing to live within the sector. By allowing this choice, government both preserves the individual's right to control his own destiny and minimizes the number of administrative minutiae and arbitrary dicta with which it must contend.

Obviously farmers judged to be young enough and with enough of the appropriate personal qualities to have a reasonably certain prospect of successful out-migration should be encouraged to do so. There would be about 28 thousand of these (Appendix A, Table A3). But if the individual chooses to remain in agriculture, even on a retired basis, he should be allowed to do so, regardless of age, as long as he does not expect special treatment under the program he chooses. (See Program 5.)

In the following outline, Program 4 is assumed to apply to all noncommercial farms, and Programs 5 and 6 are the options open to supplement Program 4. It is unlikely that Program 4 would be chosen without either Program 5 or 6 unless the individual involved had his own sources of information or other options which he could use (so that in this case he finds both Programs 5 and 6 redundant).

Further, it is assumed that Programs 4, 5, and 6 would commence concurrently with Programs 1, 2, and 3 (Chap. 5) because these latter programs have an option allowing individuals to move into Programs 4, 5, and 6 if their experience warrants it during the period in which agricultural markets become free markets.

Program 4: Facilitating Liquidation of Capital Assets on Low Income Farms

Purpose. This program is designed to insure that an individual who considers himself a noncommercial farmer can recover most of the asset value of the farm investment to which he has contributed over his lifetime. The program further has the effect of freeing resources from use so that they could be used in other farm growth, which would be part of the solution to the adjustment process for some within the agricultural sector. The administrative agent in both cases would be an appropriate government agency.

Eligibility. Any farmer would be eligible for this program, regardless of his economic class, region, or major enterprise, but no farmer would have to participate if he were willing to take the consequences of remaining in agriculture full time or on a part-time farm, under free commodity and input market conditions (after Program 3 becomes effective). Specifically, however, it would be presumed that farmers with less than $5,000 income from sales, who would not be permitted to even consider themselves as commercial farmers, and those whose farms earned $5,000-$10,000 in annual sales would participate (even though these latter farmers could opt for commercial farmer status).

Any farmer could enter this program at its inception (concurrent with Programs 1, 3, 5, or 6), or during the period of transition following the inception of the program, provided he has been enumerated as a farmer in a given census. Further, even after the transition period had ended and the agricultural sector is presumably rationalized so that viable family incomes could be earned in agriculture, individuals could opt for this program if they decide to leave agriculture.

Those who enter agriculture after the given census would do so with full knowledge of Program 3 provisions eliminating many supports and subsidies. If they fail to make a viable living in farming, they could be allowed to choose to participate in Program 4, but not 5 or 6. Since their decision to enter agriculture was made knowing that subsidies would not be paid (but that income could be stabilized), they would be considered to have made their decision at their own risk.

Transferability. The program would be for the benefit of owners of capital in agriculture, providing them with a means of converting fixed assets into liquid. Thus the programs (including 5 and 6) would not be transferable between individuals today or over generations. This means that the program would have no value which could be capitalized into asset prices. So the initial recipient would receive the full value of the program.

Time Period. This program, as well as Programs 5 and 6, would last as a continuing government policy instrument for agricultural adjustment.

Terms. Upon the farmer's initiative (either freely or after agricultural counseling) the appropriate government agency would make an offer to purchase the total assets of the farm (with the possible exception of the livestock). The offer to purchase would be at current market prices and would hold for perhaps three to six months so that the owner could test the offer against competing offers if he wished. The price would hold, even if two or three farmers in the same area should decide to liquidate simultaneously. The offer could be for the residence and the farm included, or otherwise, depending upon whether the "seller" has the idea of remaining in the house. Varying arrangements might be made with respect to the disposition of house, garden plots, and so on, so long as the farmer's intent to essentially liquidate his fixed assets is not violated. The seller, upon accepting the offer, could opt for either a lump sum payment or a series of payments over time, arranged as if the farmer owns a mortgage (the government being the mortgagee). But even in the latter case, the government agency would have the title to the assets. The possible disposition of the assets is discussed in Chapter 7. As a bonus feature, income either as a lump sum or as a series of payments under this program could possibly not be counted as income for tax purposes. In light of recent tax changes in Canada with respect to capital gains taxes, this could be a significant inducement for adjustment.

Implementation. As in Program 1, an educational program would be required to indicate the benefits both to farmers and rural communities alike, of farmers liquidating their fixed assets, which in their presently organized form do not yield a viable family income. The added advantage of several farmers being able to "sell out" without depressing asset values in the local trading area would need to be pointed out.

Lastly, the degree to which free choice with respect to supplemental programs is permitted would be emphasized. This program of education would be followed up by individual private consultation with farm families, in which the specific benefits or costs of the program could be detailed.

Administration. This program, as well as Programs 5 and 6 could be administered through the ARDA structure and financed by both federal and provincial funds. ARDA has had some experience in programs very similar to those suggested in this chapter, in fact a current ARDA program in Ontario has served as the model for this chapter's suggestions. The resources of the various provincial departments of agriculture, their staffs, as well as those in extension work (local agricultural representatives) would be required to carry out the counseling and administration involved.

Costs. Initially, a fund would be required to provide the capital for farm purchases. Assuming that the average value of assets in a farm with an annual gross income of $5,000-$7,499 is $43,000, and the average asset value of a farm earning $250-$4,999 annually is $17,500, a fund of $4.6 billion could liquidate every 1971 noncommercial farm. This is about equal in amount to the cost of ten years of agricultural programs in 1966-67, before land withholding began in Canada in the LIFT program. But even this would not be required at once, since partial payment schemes and timed withdrawal of some farmers could be planned.

Only a small part of this initial expense, even if paid at once, would be actual expense in the longer run since a supplemental program (Program 10 in Chap. 7) could provide for the resale or lease of the lands so acquired, to worthy farmers and tenants who are in the process of expansion.

Over ten years the capital liquidation program could be costless except for administration costs and the price of permanently held public lands. Once in effect, this program would preclude the need for costly partial-farm retirement programs, recently in vogue in Canada (LIFT program) or other alternate land-based supply control schemes, as described in Appendix B. A program which retires partial farms has the great disadvantage of becoming more expensive each year as land becomes more productive (when combined with machinery, fertilizers, better seed, and improved general management). This program's expense could be thought of as an insurance premium, paid to insure against the need for more stringent supply management as time and technology progress, and permitting positive supply management (Chap. 8) in addition to other national land-use policies. (See Chap. 7.)

Program 5: Farmer Retirement Supplement to Program 4

Purpose. This program is intended to supplement Program 4 by providing a means whereby low and poverty income individuals who decide (after counseling) that they would rather remain in agriculture in spite of a cancellation of subsidy programs could do so. The means suggested here give recognition to the fact that some farm families (predominantly those of older persons) may judge their cash income requirements to be low if they were allowed to have certain income in kind from their own farms.

Also, remaining in agriculture in a semiretired state may be the most efficient form of social welfare for some people, since it does not pose changes for the family involved which would create hardship.

Eligibility. All farmers enumerated in a given census (possibly 1971), who participate in Program 4 could apply for this option. While no age stipulation is made here, it might be considered desirable by some to impose one. Given the number of young farmers anticipated in low income classes in 1971 (see preceding sections of this chapter) and the terms of this present program, the participation of large numbers in this program who could reasonably be expected to successfully move to the nonfarm sector is not likely.

Terms. Once having decided to liquidate his holdings under the provisions of Program 4, a farmer could ask that he be permitted to take his payment from the government agency in a series of payments (annual, quarterly, or monthly) less an amount which would be a prearranged "rent" for house and whatever land or other assets the individual wishes to employ in farming. (Essentially this would be a sale-and-lease-back arrangement.)

If the farmer should outlive the flow of income deriving from the sale of his fixed assets, he could be given a direct income support grant to close the difference between his sales receipts, Canadian pension plan payments, and all other combined income streams, and a preassigned level of annual income judged to be fair. The chances of this contingency could be minimized by using the appropriate life expectancy tables in calculating the size of the serial payments to the farmer for his assets.

Implementation and Administration. This program would be explained as part of the education process outlined in Program 4. This program could easily be administered by ARDA in conjunction with Program 4.

Costs. In addition to the nonrecoverable outlays involved if the farm were not resold or rented after the current user had ceased to operate it, costs for income supplementation would be incurred. A specific estimate of the size of this cost is difficult to make; but it is sufficient to note that with the $1.5 billion in savings from the programs described in Chapter 5, resulting from a policy realignment, government could provide an outright gift of $9,000 per farm to all 175 thousand low income farmers. Further, the costs of welfare assistance under this plan would be lower than if no program were available because of the asset liquidation feature contained here.

Program 6: Out-Migration Supplement to Program 4

Purpose. This program would provide the means by which a farm owner in 1971 could facilitate his exit from the farm sector, having liquidated his fixed assets.

Eligibility. Farmers who had participated in Program 4, and who, after counseling, had decided to leave the sector as out-migrants would be eligible. The terms of this program would not necessarily require that the farm family vacate their house, but it would require that they give up title to virtually all but a small part of the land involved. It would seem only reasonable to try and bias the participation in this program toward persons of age thirty-five or less because of the probability that they would make a successful adjustment in this fashion. But a hard and fast rule would not be mandatory.

Terms and Provisions. The potential out-migrant would be required to fulfill the conditions of Program 4 and be allowed to choose the form in which his payment would come. He could be offered the opportunity for retraining, further education in nontechnical schools, or occupational upgrading in farm-related specialities.

The out-migrant would be eligible for placement service (as would any worker in Canada interested in changing jobs) and would be granted part or all of the dollar cost of moving if this were required.

He could also seek placement services in order to return to agriculture as a more specialized farm worker, to be employed in one or other of the growing commercial farms.

Administration and Implementation. Again, ARDA is seen as the logical choice for the administration of this program, although the cooperation of the Department of Manpower and Immigration would clearly be required. The program's implementation would be concurrent with that for Programs 4 and 5.

Costs. As in Program 5 just discussed, costs would include nonrecoverable outlays for initial farm purchases, as well as the grants required to provide retraining and relocation services. But these could be paid for out of the savings realized under programs in Chapter 5.

CONCLUSION

In total the net effect of these programs would be to quickly rationalize the use of resources within the agricultural sector by removing those resources which were in the least-productive combinations. This would have the immediate effect of reducing aggregate supply possibly by no more than 30 percent, but it would at least be a positive reduction. (In 1966, according to the Census of Agriculture, farms selling between $2,500 and $9,999 judged to be noncommercial in this context accounted for only 28.5 percent of all agricultural products sold.) The more important effect would be that farm families which were poorly rewarded by the operation of the market mechanism of agriculture would be given immediate relief without the rest of the sector experiencing the undesirable side effects which typically have accompanied efforts to remedy low incomes in the past.

The resource base of agriculture would immediately shrink under the programs suggested here, with most dramatic reductions occurring in the labor resource. The freed lands would give the government agency charged with the administration of the program a resource of its own for use in the efforts to increase the scale of potentially viable farms, or if it became public policy to do so, build a new fund of public lands for the use of the population generally.

The most important feature, however, would be that resources would be withdrawn as they are combined in full farm production units. There would not be the partial farm retirement that has characterized attempts at input control as already seen in the Canadian Prairie Provinces, and which can only lead to the augmented productivity for the fixed resources still in production within the farm unit.

All this could be achieved at minimal cost to the government under a wide set of conditions. The programs would actually break the cycle of intergeneration poverty perpetuation by forestalling the passing on of fixed farm assets from father to son, which would otherwise occur simply because there were no other alternatives.

7 Constructing an Environment for Successful Adjustment

TWO SHORTER-TERM transitional programs are presented in Chapter 5 which, if implemented, would be sufficient to set Canadian commercial agriculture on the road to achieving least-cost production, maximum competitive returns to resources, and full economic efficiency for both consumers and producers. Other features of these programs offer direct income support (on a pro rata basis) to compensate for the short-run probable losses in welfare during the transition period preceding the attainment of full economic efficiency. To attain a longer-run maintenance of income and welfare, a third program was suggested for the commercial farmers who survived the transition period. This program would remove the need to return to the kinds of commodity manipulative, income-support programs which have endured over the course of Canadian agricultural history. The programs could be implemented at a considerable saving to the Canadian treasury.

Programs presented in Chapter 6 facilitate the withdrawal of farmers and their resources, both in the present and the future, if economic conditions make it impossible for a farmer to continue producing under free market conditions. They permit a farmer to liquidate his holdings and leave the sector physically if he so chooses, or to retire while continuing to farm on a small scale. Subsidies on income, retraining, guaranteed prices for liquidated assets, assistance in relocation, and other provisions are included to complete the package. These features would remove the barriers which might otherwise restrain an individual from withdrawing from agriculture, even if he were psychologically prepared to do so. This could be done with an initial outlay, most or all of which could potentially be recovered.

But to insure that these programs both do the job for which they are intended and can themselves be phased out in part as problems disappear, an economic environment would need to be created by government policy in which ongoing adjustment could occur. That is, once the forces tending to retard the farmer's adjustment, both within and out of the sector, are overcome, government would need to initiate ongoing complementary programs designed to insure that the economic system does not trend back to its pretransition structure.

These ongoing complementary programs are of two types. The first set seeks to provide some of the kind of governmental assistance to agriculture to facilitate rapid recombination of resources (land, capital, and labor) for those who wish to grow. In addition, the programs continue government sponsorship of research, development, and extension education whenever the scale of such projects so requires. Government might reasonably expect that assistance to the development of management and technological innovation which adds to productivity and to the incomes of first adopters, be supported more by the users of the technologies directly, as if they were investing in their own expected incomes, but government still has a role in generating fundamental data in projects too extensive for private firms to finance and manage. Lastly, this set of programs suggests changes in government's political approach to farmers, and a realignment of some of the institutions which define the boundaries to the economic system within which agricultural producers function. This is, in essence, a redefinition of some of the institutional ground rules for the "game."

The second type of complementary program is required to ameliorate the side effects of agricultural adjustment as they might appear either in rural communities or within the economy as a whole, especially in agricultural commodity markets.

In total, constructing an environment for successful adjustment requires that government anticipate potential bottlenecks in the adjustment process, recognize certain rigidities in markets for inputs and products, and foresee problems created by adjustment for other parts of the economy, then take steps to eliminate the problems. It requires what Plaunt has referred to as "removing constraints on adjustment."[1]

REMOVING THE BARRIERS TO ADJUSTMENT

Since the programs of Chapter 6 address the problem of adjustment as it relates to leaving agriculture, the barriers now considered are a narrow set. What barriers might exist to adjustment within the sector after agriculture reaches the state where commodity prices are determined without withholding actions and are reflected back to producers without supports added? When costs of production are determined by the competitive market for inputs without subsidies? And yet when net income is supported and stabilized? Further, what might be the nature of these barriers? Five major elements in production—land, labor, capital, management, and desire—are reconsidered briefly, as is the institutional setting in which agriculture produces.

Personal Goals. Recalling that individuals would continue to have a choice regarding whether they wish to grow with stability, leave the sector with their accumulated capital in hand, simply remain stagnant, or become semiretired (with income support) in the sector, we see that under the programs suggested in Chapters 5 and 6 individuals' personal goals would not be frustrated. The system could accommodate all sets of private goals with equal facility. Dissemination of information about alternatives is provided under Programs 1 to 6, so that ignorance of the alternatives would not be a restraint on choice-making. So, presumably, the extent to which profit maximization was a motive in the past could remain as a motive in the future.

1. Darrel H. Plaunt, Implications of the Outlook for Adjustment, a paper presented to the Canadian Agricultural Outlook Conference, Ottawa, Nov. 1969.

Indeed, features of the program for noncommercial farmers add extra options for farmers, so that a fuller range of personal goals could be expressed. The new programs would be sufficient to remove the constraints of frustrated personal desire.

Land. Under the programs suggested in Chapters 5 and 6, control of large amounts of land would pass to the government agency involved. The same government agency would be influential in assisting the potentially viable farmers who have yet to achieve annual sales of $10,000 to enlarge their resource base. Thus, it seems that the transfer of land need not be a barrier to in-sector adjustment with the programs already suggested in effect. Still, some guidelines might be worth considering to insure the facility of transfer.

Labor. The agricultural labor force is restructured under some of the provisions suggested in earlier programs, with some individuals now operating poor farms becoming skilled, well-paid, specialized farm workers on commercial farms. But this alone could not be expected to solve the problems of labor shortages caused by seasonal fluctuations in production. Even so, it is doubtful that this would pose a real barrier to growth of commercial farms. If farms were to pay wages, offer security, and provide the fringe benefits that nonfarm firms typically pay, the labor market would respond in favor of agriculture.

But a farm's ability to provide such a wage and benefit package presupposes that labor productivity in agriculture is at least equal to that in the nonfarm sector. If this fails to be true on some farms, under the freely competitive system for agriculture envisaged, their demand for labor would decline, or investment would occur to create more productive labor, or the farm would be phased out. Even in these circumstances labor availability would not be a constraint on adjustment.

Management. The management requirements for operators of farms remaining in agriculture would likely become the major bottleneck in the adjustment process within agriculture under the programs suggested in Chapter 5 just as lack of information could be considered a major bottleneck to out-migration under the programs of Chapter 6. Of course, personal qualities of ambition and desire could also limit growth, but the lack of information and the absence of skills in handling information would even frustrate ambition. The critical role of on-farm management suggests the critical nature of continued research and extension services providing basic information and its dissemination. Whether or not government would be called upon to help relieve this barrier to adjustment is open to question and is considered further below.

Capital and Credit. With pressures for adjustment within agriculture, the growth in the size and productivity of individual farms would tend to proceed only if there is greater capital use, if only because capital is relatively more productive than labor and relatively less expensive. Capital appears to have some problems for ongoing adjustment associated with it, but what, in reality, is the capital problem? It involves knowing what capital inputs to use (i.e., given the variety of services it can perform, how to select the right mix of machines, fertilizer, seed, etc.); what should be demanded in terms of working life and capacity in machinery (i.e., given expected quality improvements, changes in crop patterns, etc.); and similar production adjustment decisions. It also requires the farmers to decide how much "capital" to actually employ (i.e., determine the firm's demand schedule for capital items).

Yet demand schedules for capital would be determined not only by the price-quantity relationships of capital alone ("At a given cost, including the rate of interest paid for its use, depreciation, maintenance, and operating expenses, how much do I buy?"). Other determinants would include the costs and benefits of capital use relative to other production inputs like land or labor (the costs of alternative means of getting similar values of output), and by the value of output itself. So the capital problem appears to be one of knowing how large the ideal capital stock should be, and what its ideal composition would be under various conditions of relative input prices and commodity prices. In other words, the capital problem is essentially a problem of management of the capital stock.

Once the management decisions concerning the size and mix of the optimal capital stock are made, a second set of management decisions would be required concerning the acquisition or disposal of capital, that is, a set of investment decisions. But the investment decision would depend on what the individual farmer judges to be his preferences for current rather than future income (resulting from the return on the investment), and the perceived ability of his farm to yield a return in the future if investment occurs today. (This is simply a restatement of the well-accepted basis of intertemporal resource allocation—investment today for future income—given by Irving Fisher, in which productivity and thrift determine current investment.) Naturally, an individual may accept the going market rate of interest as a determinant of the degree to which he prefers future to present income, but it need not be the only determinant. Even so, the investment decision would still be an individual's management decision concerning his demand for investment funds.

For capital, and hence investment funds, to be a barrier to adjustment, supplies of capital and investment funds would have to be less than the demands for them at a cost farmers would be willing to pay. But if this were the case there would be excessive demands for capital in agriculture at current rates. Clearly, this is not consistent with observable fact.

What would more likely be true is that as the farmer population generally grows older (a tendency shown in Appendix A) they prefer lower debts, even though they know that they could get credit. The compulsion to own a debt-free farm probably influences investment preferences, so that credit management practices which made good economic sense in the early years of farming (i.e., incurring debt to earn income at a higher rate than the rate of interest to be paid, and so realizing a profit) would no longer be employed.

This hypothesis is strongly supported by studies conducted in Iowa[2] where a survey was made, covering farms in crop, beef, swine, and general categories, whose operators had been farming an average of nineteen years and were about forty-two years of age. Farms were classified by income class (in $10,000 intervals from $0). With a proportion of net in gross income of 0.30, an Iowa farm of between $15,000 and $20,000 would be relatively as well off as a Canadian farm in the $10,000 gross income class. Of the 172 farms surveyed, 13 earned less than $10,000 gross income and another 43 earned between $10,000 and $20,000. This study can, at least, suggest a hypothesis about the likely behavior of Canadian commercial farmers. Farmers surveyed were asked—

1. How much money they could borrow if they wished (to determine the individual's assessment of the limits imposed on him by both the market and his own preferences).
2. How much outstanding liability they have (an indication of willingness to incur debt).

If the average answer to (1) was less than or equal to the average answer to (2), the survey would indicate that lines of credit were generally exhausted. But if (2) was less than (1), no case could be validly made for the view that credit is a generally limiting factor in farm growth.

In no income class did the average outstanding liability exceed 50 percent of the credit that the farmers in that class knew they could get, or (and this is more important) would have been willing to take if prevailing interest rates and other cost levels had been the only determinant of their demand for investment funds.

Obviously an individual farmer would be unwise not to shop for the lowest possible rate of interest and terms when he decides to make a capital purchase. A farm group or lobby would probably be serving their

2. As yet unpublished study at Iowa State University: I.S.U. Project 1616 by A. G. Ball, Selected Elements in the Growth of the Farm Firm.

own best interests if they tried to recruit the government to help in the "dickering" for lower credit costs or to provide a credit at subsidized rates. But capital subsidies would only accelerate the rate of capital purchase on well-managed and progressive farms, a rate which would be high even without the subsidy, because the personal qualities of the manager would likely be such as to favor investment. On the other hand, such subsidies would have no impact on the managers like the average manager in the Iowa study, who did not even exhaust the possible sources of credit he knew about.

Clearly then, the capital problem would more probably be a problem of capital management than capital shortage. Any lack of capital use in agriculture could reasonably be attributed to the lack of management's desire to use credit than to any other cause. Again, this applies to commercial farms in our sense of the word. For those farms which are noncommercial and will withdraw from agriculture, no capital problem exists, since they will not grow and would have liquidated their existing capital stock, or a large part of it, under Program 4 (Chap. 6). But capital supply is not likely to be a barrier to adjustment under the new programs.

Institutions. The analysis of Chapter 3 demonstrates that as long as government legitimizes proposed action by instigators at a micro, grass-roots level, the political process would continue to culminate in the adoption of commodity-oriented subsidies, input price subsidies, and legalized compulsory supply-withholding actions. This follows because, at the grass-roots level, the perceived common bonds between farmers are sameness of commodity, and not sameness of basic economic income and adjustment problems. The political process itself could easily continue to be a barrier to adjustment, for if government continues to legitimize actions for social change on the commodity level, it will be inviting continued pressure for more commodity-based programs.

Plaunt has also observed these institutional barriers to adjustment.[3] He describes the barrier which exists because of the fragmentation of the "farm block" along commodity and regional lines, the resultant fragmentation of agricultural policy development (always seeking but never finding solutions to fundamental economic problems of farmers), and "the difficulties in mobilizing the contributions of farm organizations . . . to agricultural adjustment," in part because farm groups still believe that they can have their own pet projects legitimized without the cooperation of other farm groups. So there are barriers to adjustment in the way in which government has become accustomed to dealing with the agricultural sector, which should be altered.

In summary, therefore, it appears that the major economic barriers to adjustment within agriculture under programs in Chapters 5 and 6 would be management barriers. Once the management level increases, many of the problems of resource allocation, especially capital and credit problems, would become minimal. What is recommended in the following section is a set of programs to assist farm management to become more competent. Unlike those in Chapters 5 and 6, these programs will not be detailed, nor will costs be estimated. Besides, these programs are of secondary importance in relation to those given above. Further, many are now in existence in other forms.

In addition, there is the political barrier to adjustment which was described in Chapter 3 which also could be removed. We recall that this barrier was that resulting from farmers' organizing primarily on a commodity basis, their owing allegiance to a commodity-oriented organization, and their not being discouraged from seeking narrow programs aimed at commodities and inputs. In fact with a decline in rural population and continued redistribution of electoral seats in favor of urban areas, there should be every natural encouragement for removal of the barrier.

3. Plaunt, Outlook for Adjustment, p. 18.

PROGRAMS TO OVERCOME THE BARRIERS

The systems proposed in Chapters 5 and 6 create a situation in which an individual could achieve his own set of personal goals without frustration. The programs do not require that an individual necessarily reshape his goals in order to benefit from them. His own goals and personal qualities, therefore, would not be a barrier to his adjustment, either within agriculture or as one who chooses to withdraw (out-migration, or quasi-retirement). Yet with the less-than-perfect knowledge an individual has of his own real goals, his personal and imposed limitations, or the system that he faces, the set of alternatives from which he can choose narrows. Hence, even though the system allows for considerable freedom of choice, information about and understanding of these programs would be vital before a wise choice could be made.

This recognition leads to the following suggested program:

Program 7: Rationalization and Revitalization of Agricultural Information Systems. With about 4.5 percent of all government expenditures (about $21 million in 1966-67) spent on extension, and another 2 percent spent on education and grants to agricultural schools (Table 1.1), information is currently being moderately well distributed in Canadian agriculture. The question should be asked, however, how one can eliminate the expense of publishing and spreading information of marginal use in the process of adjustment, while giving full information (such as that required for Programs 1-6) upon which rational individual choices can be made with respect to adjustment alternatives.

Extension and education is largely a provincial matter. A revised information program could simply consist of an internal study of the relative costs and benefits of all communications media (publications, radio or television coverage, personal contact, public meetings, etc.) and allocate a higher budget to those media which have the greatest benefits as compared to costs. The relevant benefits and costs would be judged as the affected goal of adjustment. Departments might even consider appointing an internal director of media and information to keep budget allocations working in the most effective way. Much technical expertise in this field is undoubtedly available in the business and the professional media worlds which could be tapped.

A program such as Program 7 would require that information be already available with an audience in mind. Part of the necessary information and its audience has been described in Chapters 5 and 6, and would deal with the choice of whether to remain in agriculture. But for those who remain, another kind of information would be needed: namely, the management information, which is derived from research efforts.

Program 8: Rationalization and Increasing Research Efforts in Fundamental Questions of Production and Management. In the adjustment process as envisaged in Chapters 5 and 6, the demand for information would come from three sources: the commercial farmers who already have in excess of $10,000 gross sales per year, the aspirant commercial farmers who are now under forty-five years of age and earning between $5,000 and $10,000 in gross sales, and finally the noncommercial farmers, who would be out-migrants and semiretired.

Obviously, little economic, productive, or managerial advice would be required by the latter group, although some advice as to the management of their liquid assets derived from the sale of their fixed assets and the management of a small noncommercial farm might minimize the burden of withdrawal for those involved. The out-migrants would already have the advice they need concerning job placement and actual moving.

The aspirant commercial farmers, however, would require both production and management services with a strong emphasis on the management aspect. The advice would have to be tailored specifically for an individual farmer with his initial resources and other attributes, and would probably be concentrated in the areas of capital management, general production management, and planning. The commercial farmers probably need less intensive management advice in production-oriented fields, but could probably use capital management advice (see Program 9).

Most management advice derives from more basic research into the economics of resource allocation, optimal production patterns, and of basic physical growth relationships in livestock and crops. Thus there would be two stages in the promotion and realignment of research efforts—the development of fundamental data and its translation into usable decision rules for farms.

The latter step in the process—translation of basic research findings into usable decision rules—is now in its embryonic stages in Canada, particularly in the public sector, in the form of Canadian Farm Management Data Systems (CANFARM), in Guelph, Ontario. Such efforts could never be oversupported, for with expanded funding, such a service could conceivably provide individual management advice to each commercial farmer throughout his adjustment process.

Indeed, expanded funding could come in part from the charging of a small fee prorated by the size of income of the farm. This could be justifiable on the grounds that the user would derive significant benefits from the advice, and should be willing, as well as able, to pay for it.

But while there is reason to believe that the demands for an institution to spread management services specific enough to be useful to growing farms could be met, the fundamental research effort in Canada does not appear to be aligned with the expected need for economic and farm management information. For, as Table 7.1 illustrates, most research—37 percent—is conducted in the area of plant production and protection, 15 percent in livestock production and protection, and only 7 percent for the basic economic studies which could immediately translate into applied management.

Not only would the basic research effort as it now stands tend to be less useful as an underpinning of economic management advice for commercial farmers, but it offers practically no help in managing the withdrawal of 175 thousand noncommercial farmers. Studies that generate the information that would help in this

Table 7.1. Allocation of Professional Research Staffs in Canada, 1967, by Discipline, in Man-Years

Discipline	Total Man-Years	Percentage of Grand Total	Expenditure ($ million)
Natural sciences			
Plant production and protection	545.9	36.9	...
Animal production and protection	219.1	14.8	...
Other	555.4	37.5	...
Subtotal	1,320.4	89.2	61.6
Agricultural engineering			
Machinery	16.4	1.1	...
Power, structures and environmental control	6.3	0.5	...
Crop, food processing	1.5	0.1	...
Materials, water resources, and soils	15.2	1.0	...
Research equipment	2.9	0.2	...
Subtotal	42.3	2.9	5.2
Agricultural economics			
Economic development	3.9	0.3	...
Economics of production	54.1	3.6	...
Marketing, distribution, and trade	18.3	1.2	...
Resource use and development	10.3	0.7	...
Agricultural policy	4.8	0.3	...
Cooperatives	2.9	0.2	...
Methodology and theory, economics, and interregional competition	4.0	0.2	...
Subtotal	98.8	6.5	7.1
Sociology			
Anthropology and social psychology	4.3	0.2	...
General sociology	10.1	0.7	...
Rural sociology	6.5	0.4	...
Extension	1.0	0.1	...
Subtotal	22.1	1.4	0.8
Total	1,483.6	100.0	74.7

Source: Compiled from Federal Task Force on Agriculture, Canadian Agriculture in the Seventies (Ottawa: Queen's Printer, 1970), p. 399.

regard, based on psychology and rural sociology, account for only 1.4 percent of the research effort.

Thus the new direction in agricultural research suggested in this program should aim for (1) increase in the basic research effort in economic studies, which are related eventually to management applications—not necessarily at the dollar expense of research in natural sciences, (2) increased sociological inquiries into the effects of migration, job mobility, and early retirement of individuals of various ages and incomes, and (3) a refining of the management services offered (such as the CANFARM system).

Of all the resources used in agriculture, the capital resource appears to be the most misused. But studies have suggested that the supply side of the capital market, and hence the investment funds market, could not be considered the likely cause of "the capital problem." Rather, if farmers who wish to invest (and not all do, continually, throughout their farming lives) knew better how and when to use funds and where to get them (i.e., if they were better managers of capital), the problem might not even appear to exist. With better capital management the creation of new credit agencies would seem to serve little purpose, except to eliminate some duplication and give the appearance that there were fewer, but not necessarily more willing, sources of funds. To suggest that there is a need for a federal-provincial credit board to supersede all existing lending institutions (presumably, to provide more credit to commercial agriculture and small farmers at lower than market rates), seems to assume that demand is currently pressing hard on supply at existing market rates. Evidence of this in Canada is not strong. (This was a recommendation of the Federal Task Force on Agriculture. There appears to be some inconsistency in their recommendations, for in addition to this "super board," which would in effect force easier credit conditions for agriculture, the Task Force also recommends the removal of subsidies from agricultural capital. The latter suggestion would be consistent with the conclusion reached in our Chapter 2; the former would not.)

Under the proposed schemes in Chapter 6 and Program 10 below, credit in the form of mortgages for farm expansion could be a simple matter to arrange between the farmer and the land adjustment agency. If the agency rented out rather than sold the land to a farmer wishing to use it, no long-term credit problem would exist. Operating capital (short-term credit) would come more fully from commercial banks, which could be encouraged with some financial help to develop expertise in recognizing good farm and capital management, to deemphasize "collateral" requirements, and generally to increase their participation in agricultural business enterprises.

But all the concern over capital supply merely begs the fundamental point that the capital problem is a capital management problem to which the following program is directed:

Program 9: Improvement of the Quality of Capital Management in Agriculture. The compulsion for the debt-free farm, or the psychological barrier against jeopardizing the ownership of the "family's farm" might easily restrain many from seeking more investment funds. This, of course, is a matter of personal choice and preference, and not subject to laws or regulations. For those who wish it, however, specialized capital management services could be dispersed in addition to general farm management information through CANFARM or extension representatives.

Special efforts should be made not only to educate farmers with respect to use of capital, but also sources of capital. With encouragement, commercial banks might be persuaded to perform functions now filled by high-priced credit agencies connected with machinery dealers, seed dealers, and other purchased nonfarm inputs. The encouragement might be in the form of loss insurance which could be bought from the government by the borrower.

Part of agriculture's presumed credit problem stems from the traditional need for mortgages to facilitate farm acreage growth. However, provisions of Program 10 would eliminate this problem.

Program 10: Rationalization of National Land Use. At

least three countries now have national policies to allow public acquisition of land from private farmers for purposes of making farm operations conform with national desires and objectives. Sweden's program has been in operation for several years and requires that if the present farmer wishes to sell his holdings, the land be sold (unless permission is otherwise granted) to a designated district or county land authority. The local organization specifies to whom the land can be resold under a set of preassigned priorities reflecting national policy. Priority is given to operators of small or undersized units with prospects of further growth. Holland requires that all farmers who leave their units to enter the retraining program or the early retirement program sell their farms to the public authority, which then decides the nature of resale, with emphasis being given to the enlargement of small farms and use of land for public purposes such as recreation. New legislation written in 1967 in the United Kingdom provides for a similar acquisition and resale operation by government.

Under the provisions of Programs 4 and 5, a Canadian public agency (presumed to be ARDA) would acquire farms from noncommercial farmers who are leaving agriculture. The agency would, under Program 5, take title to the land and then lease it back for the rent of the operator's lifetime. Under this program the agency would have the power to sell, lease, or simply accumulate public lands.

In the case of outright sale provisions, the agency could recoup the outlay made for the land, and assume the mortgagor's position, thus solving the purchaser's long-term credit problem. The agency would have the power to decide on the eligibility of and priority given to different buyers. Priority might be given to buyers who meet certain criteria in respect to (1) farm size (those smaller than the size prescribed for adequate income and efficient operation) and (2) sufficient capital and management resources for success. Existing farm operators who wish and need to enlarge their units could apply for purchases. Those having the greatest promise of success, based on the second criterion, would be certified as eligible and could be allowed to bid on land acquired by the land authority. Or the agency could simply select the operator judged to have the greatest chance for success based on his training, experience, capital availability, and a test of his managerial ability. The latter method, with some modification in priority, is used in Holland to select farm families to be settled on the new land holdings.

As an added feature outside the realm of the current discussion, the land authority also could be commissioned to actively buy land for permanent conversion to other uses. These powers could be merged with those relating to the development and settlement of new lands or irrigation investment. Depending on the instrument finally selected to remedy general income problems, the land authority could be empowered to buy up land and withhold it from crop production or shift it to noncrop uses.

The agency could also lease the land as a permanent arrangement or as a prelude to a sale after the "experiment" with leasing proved successful. Criteria similar to those for an outright sale could be used. This latter course is very close to the currently effective ARDA program in Ontario.

Another alternative would be for the agency to simply hold the land. The net acquisition function would serve several purposes, not the least of which would be to partially control output potential. Farmers selling their holdings would probably be the poorest, and it is recognized that the poorest 30 percent of Canadian farmers add only 10 percent to the total value of production.[4] Even so, this means of output control through land withholding could rank relatively high among other alternate land-based control systems if it were conducted on a full-farm basis as shown in Appendix B.

Any of the above schemes could serve broader national interests: they could be used to control the ownership of Canadian farmlands by foreigners (a cur-

4. W. L. Porteous, Canadian Farm Income Levels and Distribution, a paper presented to the Canadian Agricultural Outlook Conference, Ottawa, Nov. 1969.

rently popular and not entirely unreasoned motive), to enlarge recreational areas, or simply to forestall irreversible land-use practices (like highway strip development and habitation sprawl in areas without zoning ordinances or proper facilities for living). The passage of title from one citizen to another through an open forum rather than through private transition may be considered an invasion of privacy, but with this would be associated a gain in solving problems before they arise and become unsolvable.

Even though labor availability would not be a bottleneck to the agricultural adjustment of commercial farms within agriculture directly, the withdrawal of farmers from agriculture could be hampered if adequate assistance to overcome the natural reluctance and ability barrier to mobility is not available. A slower rate of out-migration would slow the rate at which lands could be acquired and thus retard, in an indirect way, the rate at which commercial farmers could grow.

Program 11: Expansion of Retraining, Relocation, and Assistance Programs. The main elements of this program have been outlined as part of Program 6 in Chapter 6. The need for retraining for those who could migrate to nonfarm jobs, to offer financial support for their physical moves, to counsel them to lower their personal costs of adjustment, and to help out-migrants convert their capital and savings from farm-bound assets into liquid assets was outlined. In at least one province—Ontario—ARDA has had such a program under way for about five years in conjunction with the Federal Department of Manpower and Immigration. In the Ontario scheme, many out-migrants retrain and return to other, larger agricultural enterprises as specialized farm workers whose productivity earns high wages. Similar activity to assist in the placement and training of out-migrants could readily be expanded into all provinces, with interprovincial mobility encouraged.

It was noted earlier that programs for regional development, like FRED and ADA projects, would assist the farm labor and migration problem by stimulating growth in nonfarm or farm-related industry in previously agricultural regions. This would naturally reduce many of the costs of out-migration which would otherwise be borne by the migrant or the government. But by their very nature, FRED and ADA projects can serve only selected localities. By contrast the ARDA program could assist agriculture specifically in all parts of the country. Therefore Program 10 advocates, in effect, the extension of manpower services, already well developed in the nonfarm sector, to the farm sector as well, with recognition of the unique problems of out-migrants.

Eventually, in the discussion of what program additions or deletions might be considered for implementation, the question arises as to what would be practical in the sense of what is or could be made politically acceptable. It becomes a matter of knowing what other changes would have to be made in order to make the original proposals "practical." (The changes proposed so far are practical in the sense that they identify and are consistent with the true cause and effect of the situations involved; that is, the proposals would work if accepted.)

One could suggest that the need indicated by the programs proposed in this book is for more education for farmers, to show them the folly of asking for commodity- and input-based programs by demonstrating to them the logic in Chapter 2. One could also suggest that this be followed by instruction in what logic lies behind the types of programs suggested in Part 2 and the likelihood of favorable outcomes from these alternate programs. But this would be neither feasible nor workable, although one might hope that as this logic is recognized and taught in schools oriented toward agricultural education, the ideas might seep through into the body of commonly accepted wisdom.

Government itself would have to do nothing more to facilitate the changes recommended here than to use the political processes to set a framework in which farm groups themselves would form more cohesive and significantly noncommodity-based unions; which in turn would eventually ask for and support direct income-related programs, and noncommodity-based adjustment programs.

The argument of Chapter 3 attempts to show that by allowing itself to succumb to pressure by small, grassroots level, commodity-oriented groups, government essentially defines rules within whose bounds commodity-oriented legislation had to emerge. On the other hand, if government would permit itself to be pressured only by provincial, regional, or even national spokesmen for farmers, then farmers would out of necessity find a basis for organizations of such scope among themselves without further urging. Farmers would organize along the lines that the government permitted to be politically effective, and in the process of internal compromise and struggle, farmers would come to recognize the commonalities in their income problems apart from their types of enterprise. They could then be counted upon to support programs similar to those outlined above (Chap. 5 and 6).

One would not have to recommend the creation of a new proliferation of "boards," which at best merely define points of positional leadership only coincidentally connected to the real power structure.[5] Farmers would form the groups they felt would work in the circumstances.

It is no doubt an interesting and abstract academic problem to determine whether there are too many farm organizations, or what form agricultural organizations ought to take in order to achieve some purpose or other. But in reality, optimal forms of politically motivated bodies generally are not normative in nature. The process of reshaping the power structure, once new rules of a political system are defined, would automatically give the number and structure of farm organizations which would be consistent with the implicit and fundamental goals of farmers themselves. An attempt to prescribe the structure "as it ought to be" would essentially be an attempt to prescribe a normative set of goals for farmers.

---

5. Unfortunately, the Federal Task Force took this approach; see Federal Task Force on Agriculture, Canadian Agriculture in the Seventies (Ottawa: Queen's Printer, 1970), p. 291.

The definition of a set of communications channels, meeting schedules, lists of participants, and rankings among participants probably constitutes a more interesting theoretical exercise in textbook business administration than a realistic recommendation for involving more farmers in the process of political policy making. If any legislated or forcibly organized system fails to coincide with the channels, schedules, participants, and rank among participants in the actual power structure, it would merely define a set of procedural roadblocks to effective policy making and create further barriers to adjustment.

Policy making could be more realistically viewed as a competition between conflicting desires in a political setting. Hence, policy would emerge which favors the strongest competitor, the competitor with the most power. But power is based on vote control, money, personalities of leaders, and not mere position (and has the essential quality that when used, it forces things to go in favor of the power holder's goals, regardless of who holds what formal position). Any proposed change in the positions of persons for the purpose of policy coordination which fails to reflect this would offer farmers no better means of influencing national agricultural policy than they now have.

Yet, even if a detailed study were conducted, which undertook to identify the power structure as it is and prescribe the channels, meeting schedules, participants, and rank among participants to precisely reflect it, there would be a simpler way of achieving the same thing. Realizing this is the motivation for Program 12.

Program 12: Adjustment of the Institutional Framework for Policy Making. The adjustment deemed necessary for the success of ongoing adjustment would be away from a set of institutions which favor continued political foment for commodity-oriented programs toward a set of institutions concerned with problems of income, welfare, and adjustment, specifically and directly.

The need would be not for a specific program incorporated in legislation, but more of a change in the bias of government leadership in the operation of policy making. Provincial governments, for example, could let it be known in more or less subtle terms that they would willingly recognize and listen to representatives from one provincial farmers' union alone rather than from twenty producer groups organized on a commodity basis. The federal government could indicate by a few decisions that it would recognize one national spokesman organization (or even three or four regional ones) and then simply wait for the result, a process that occurred in the United Kingdom before national farmers' organizations were formed.

Governments would not have to ban existing groups or force their confederation and would definitely not legislate the creation of new organizations since such new creations would probably neither represent the existing power structure within agriculture nor permit the free formation of groups with the structure and membership consistent with farmers' individual goal attainment processes. Such creations would merely cloud the scene with more titles and powerless positions.

There are already two national organs—the Canadian Federation of Agriculture and the National Farmers' Union—and a number of provincial farmers' unions, so that it might appear as if Program 12 suggests nothing new. But these federal and provincial unions are already developed, and formed in a time when government allowed wheat producers, hog producers, dairymen, vegetable growers, to name a few, to petition government independently as well as through the union structure. Thus, today's farmer unions and federations in effect are competing with the specific commodity groups for membership and power. Hence, under the current structure, the farmer unions and federations must pressure for specific commodity programs in order to appease the commodity factions within their membership, lest these farmers exercise their options and abandon the union, putting their full support behind specific commodity groups instead. Program 12 suggests that government close off completely (or at least seriously discount) the option of pressuring government through the commodity group, as an alternate to a more general union. The result would be farmer unions or federations with real farmer support and power, supporting a set of programs and expressed goals more directly related to farm income and adjustment problems than at present.

The argument to this point should not be taken as an advocacy of the current farmers' union concept, or the present farmers' union leadership, membership methods, constitution, or programs. Program 12 simply points at the need for a new "farm block" structure as an effective instrument for achieving farm income and adjustment goals, and shows what would have to be done to create the new structure. Undoubtedly, parts of the old power structure (current leaders, membership, constitutions, and so on) would survive the transition and be part of the new structure. This would be neither necessary nor necessarily desirable; it would just be a fact of life.

ALLEVIATING HARDSHIPS ON RURAL COMMUNITIES

The amount of research effort and funds spent on rural sociology relative to other categories of agriculture-related topics (Table 7.1) indicates a low level of study of the side effects of agricultural policy on the rural communities. In 1967, only 1.4 percent of all professional man-years spent on Canadian agriculture was devoted to the study of sociology, in comparison with 89.2 percent devoted to studying the developments which tend to create sociological problems for rural people (i.e., growth in productivity of plants and animals).

Some of the policies proposed in this volume to solve the problems of farmers, both commercial and noncommercial, would aggravate the problems of rural towns. The trend toward fewer farms and a smaller agricultural labor force would have effects on the small towns serving such communities, not unlike those impinging on noncommercial farms. Thus, with declining volumes of business, declining ability, and declining desire of proprietors to undertake the investments and make the management decisions necessary to "keep up," the out-migration of more able young people and the tendency in the rural population's age distribution to be skewed toward the old, rural communities would decline as agriculture transforms. Essentially, reduced farm populations would have an adverse effect on recreational facilities, welfare programs, education, income levels and its distribution, and the quality of small town life in general. In a downward spiral, if an exogenous economic shock occurs to the town which places it in financial difficulty, it responds by reducing the level of services it offers, which in turn makes the town a relatively poorer place in which to live. Under this stimulus other businesses and people leave, eroding the tax base and creating more financial trouble, and so on. Thus all rural people, farmers and townspeople, should be included in a policy framework designed to alleviate and solve the problems stemming from the rapid technological, organizational, and institutional transformation of agriculture.

The answer, however, is not in abandoning the agricultural policies which would actually solve agriculture's problems. Rather, it lies in identifying some of the points of greatest pressure created by agricultural adjustment in rural towns and dealing with them. To do otherwise would be like "throwing out the baby with the bath water." The nature of these pressure points could be predicted, based on available evidence from previously studied agricultural areas in flux.[6] Then the specific changes which might be expected in a rural town can be treated as (1) farm population declines, (2) transportation technology progresses and roads improve, and (3) agricultural programs such as those proposed here tend to speed the rate at which out-migration occurs.

Model of Rural Social Change. Suppose a hypothetical geographic region contained, in the past, three or four central towns or other localities at a time when trade in the region could maintain each place as a "partial" or "complete" shopping center.[7] The kind of

---

6. See, for example, K. A. Fox and T. K. Kumar, Delineating Functional Economic Areas, in Research and Education for Regional and Area Development, Iowa State University Center for Agricultural and Economic Development (Ames: Iowa State Univ. Press, 1966), pp. 13-55.

7. Ibid., p. 46.

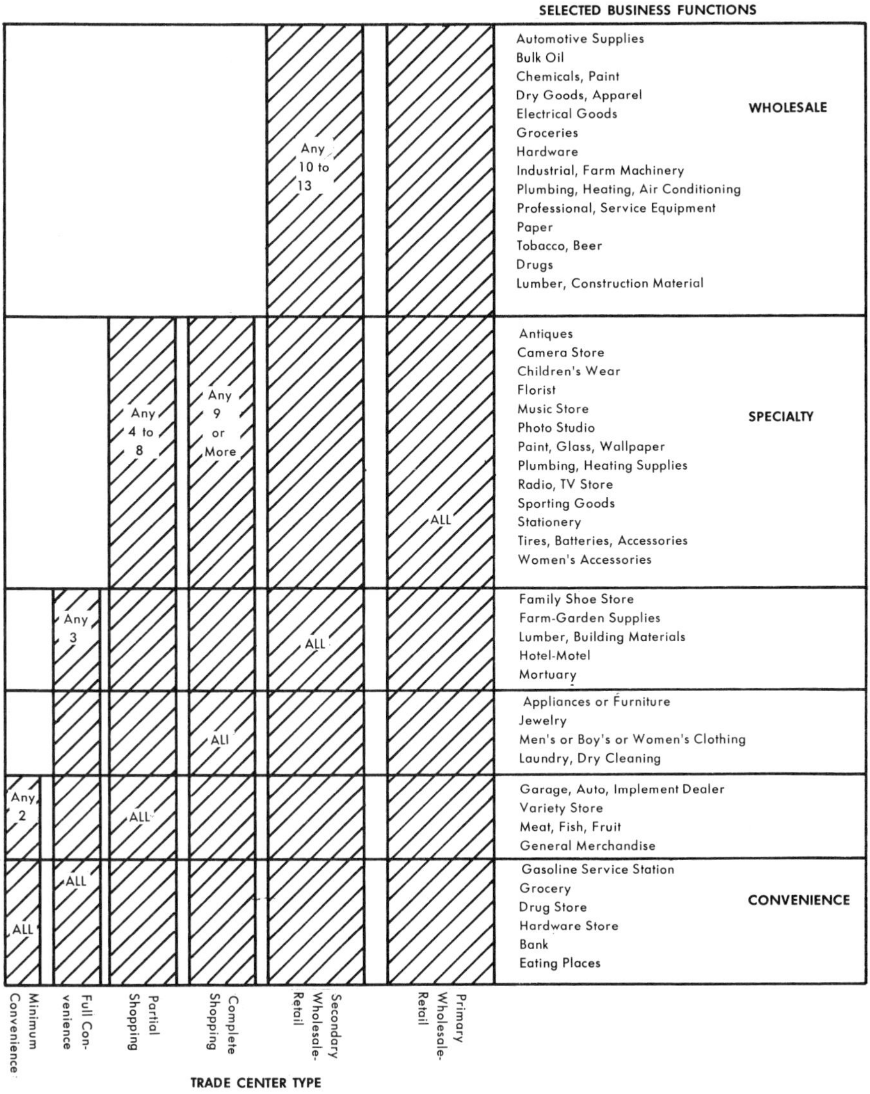

FIG. 7.1. Trade center types defined by business functions. Businesses which are required and optional in defining each type of trade center are indicated by markings on each bar. Width of bar is proportional to dollar volume for partial shopping centers and above. From Karl A. Fox and T. Krishna Kumar, Delineating functional economic areas, in Research and Education for Regional and Area Development, CAED (Ames: Iowa State Univ. Press, 1966).

economic activity that would possibly be found in these centers is indicated in Figure 7.1. These might include a wide range of business establishments, both convenience (gasoline station, bank, drug store) and speciality (florist, sporting goods store).

But as travel improves or as population declines (farm or nonfarm) the economic rationalization of the area might dictate that some of the centers survive only as "full convenience centers." For with improved travel, customers could commute farther in a given time and could choose to purchase speciality items in the same place and time as they purchase wholesale items, thus saving trips. As the population in the previous trade area declines, the volume of business feeding the speciality shops would decline. Eventually, both forces could remove the need for as many specialized shops as previously existed, some of which would go out of business. Thus there would be an evolution in central places—some growing, others declining.

These would be "natural forces," which could occur—in fact, have occurred—regardless of national policy. But as national agricultural policy accelerates the rate of population decline in rural areas, decline of some servicing communities would be speeded, forcing proprietors to adjust or go out of business within their productive lifetimes. Formerly, natural forces may have only convinced a son not to take up his father's business, while permitting the father to live out his life in this business. Under more rapid agricultural transformation, the father himself would be under pressure to adjust. Thus, as some central localities become "full convenience" or "partial convenience" centers, or even cease to exist at all, under the spur of agricultural adjustment the proprietors of businesses which are no longer economically justified would be faced with the same problems that face aging or low income farmers. They would be forced to accept a deterioration in real income, a real income that is decreasing at a faster rate than "normal." There are fewer opportunities to leave the community because of their age or recoup their investments in their businesses. When two or three or even more individuals in the same town undergo similar pressures simultaneously, the outlook for the town itself is bleak.

This model generally describes the process which has been observed in much of rural Canada. It describes in addition some of the tendencies, already well known, between competing regions. Thus, even untested with empirical evidence in this study, the model can be accepted intuitively as describing Canadian problems. It suggests several elements which would be necessary in any program designed to mitigate the side effects of agricultural adjustment.

Elements of the Policy. Yielding to the temptation to institute programs with the goal of reversing the process of community adjustment, possibly out of some misplaced humanitarian instinct, would be a grave error. Such programs would be futile in the long run because the economic forces creating agricultural adjustment are macro-economic in scope and could not be altered with sector-oriented or community-oriented programs. To try and reverse the trends would only hold out false hope to the people involved, would merely postpone the day when the adjustment would eventually have to be made, and deny them much needed help in the short run.

This is not to say, however, that slowing the trends so that older people in rural communities could live out their lives comfortably without having to undertake the financial or psychic costs of adjustment, or so that towns could undertake adjustment at a slower rate, lacks economic reason. Provided the direction of the trend is clearly identified and persons are not misled into believing that growth is possible where decline is inevitable, adjustment to a slower rate of change would probably be less costly than adjustment to a faster rate. Thus, programs such as those suggested in Chapter 6 under which farmers could liquidate their assets but remain residents in their traditional communities would have spin-off benefits for the rural towns in traditional trade areas. No one who is familiar with the terms of the "retired" farmers' tenancies would be led to believe that a decline in the rural population is not inevitable. But knowing with greater certainty the rate at which the decline would occur would grant the town population the necessary time to undertake their own least-cost adjustment.

Possibly, programs similar to those proposed for noncommercial farmers might be considered for specific individuals who could not adjust even to the slowed rate of change in declining towns. Eventually, however, decisions must be made by government and the people involved concerning whether a geographic location has become too small to warrant further support as an independent town. At this point economies of scale in community organization could be sought through community consolidation. Government assistance in this regard would be required in the form of financing, counseling, and relief to the dispossessed.

These tendencies and ideas have been long recognized within the Canadian setting, as is evident in the attempts of various provinces to assist community redevelopment on more economically justified scales. Indeed, some projects financed through the Fund for Regional Economic Development have been successful in revitalizing whole regions by exploiting new economic opportunities and adding new scale to traditional communities. Adjustment of commercial agriculture would go far in helping these successes to materialize and remain viable over time. Redevelopment, however, would not be a reasonable prospect for all rural regions, because not all regions have advantages that can be exploited with economic soundness. Not all towns are potential growth centers, nor do all politically defined regions or groups of counties necessarily contain growth centers, even if rural industrialization might offer a partial solution to the problems created by agricultural adjustment for selected rural communities. Thus, policy for total rural redevelopment must not only plan for the growth in some regions or communities, but also for the orderly and least-cost demise of others.[8]

---

8. See an expansion of these concepts in Iowa State University Center for Agricultural and Economic Development, Benefits and Burdens of Rural Development (Ames: Iowa State Univ. Press, 1970).

CONCLUSION

A set of supporting programs has been suggested in this chapter to insure that the economic pressures causing the current adjustment problems for agriculture would not frustrate the positive benefits of the revised programs. Since adjustment, either within the sector or without, would require knowledge and skill, the supplemental programs have the effect of providing it. Since the current morass of agricultural programs is a result of a government attitude toward the farm sector as a political entity, the chapter has suggested a possible change in the attitude.

The side effects of agricultural adjustment on rural communities have also been considered and a similarity observed in the problems of the poor rural town merchant and the low income farmer. Both would face problems as a result of the transformation of agriculture; both would tend to lose personal welfare and value of assets; and both would be subjected to the rigors of forced migration or poverty. Programs for the low income segment of rural communities could follow the pattern of programs envisaged for the low income section of the farming community.

8 Policies for Ongoing Supply Management

IN 1966, according to data in the Census of Agriculture, if all the producers offering less than $10,000 in products on commodity markets had ceased production, total output would have declined by only 35 percent. Further, if the policies suggested in Part 2 of this book were implemented—that is, if all the farms offering less than $5,000 in products for sale were to phase themselves out with no reuse of their resources, total output would decline by only 11 percent. This alone is sufficient to indicate that ongoing farm adjustment policies conducted without supply management measures would be increasingly difficult and costly to enforce. It also suggests that farm adjustment programs alone will not solve the problems of excess supply potential in agriculture.

Interpreted literally, the phrase "supply management" could mean both a decrease of the supply of commodities offered for sale when they are in "surplus" (relative to demand at more or less stable prices) and a planned increase of the supply of commodities with high or rising prices (lessening inflation). Both interpretations would be relevant to and consistent with the programs given in Chapters 5 and 6. The more conventional meaning of supply management, that of withholding supply, or "negative" supply management, would clearly still have significance, even with freed markets supported and incomes stabilized. The cost of these programs could rise rapidly if prices fluctuated widely and randomly. With uncertainty, consumers' welfare itself would suffer because they would be forced to take steps to minimize the costs of price instability.

On the other hand, the enactment of positive supply management programs would add both speed and certainty to the responses of farmers to projected and actual commodity shortages. "Shortages" could be indicated by price rises at the farm level, or by forecasts of new developments in varieties, markets, or tastes. This presumes that at present some positive supply response warranted by price and exceptional incentives does not occur because of uncertainty created for prices and income if all farmers respond equally, if forecasts are in error, if the projected period of shortages is too short to yield sufficient income to cover change-over costs, and so on.

Farmers themselves would not have to fear planning to increase selected commodities for, under Programs 1 and 2, they would be compensated for changes in income resulting from changed market conditions and would have their incomes stabilized at levels consistent with their "historic" welfare level. Under the proposed programs of Chapter 5, commercial farmers' incomes would not be determined solely by market prices or (by inference) levels of production. Therefore, if programs to support and stabilize incomes are to be effective, both positive and negative supply management would be warranted.

This chapter largely deals with problems which are associated with ongoing commercial agriculture. The programs for noncommercial farmers would in effect remove them from agriculture now and over time as they age and retire. Their interests would be well served by the programs of Chapter 6 alone.

PROGRAMS TO IMPLEMENT POSITIVE SUPPLY MANAGEMENT

Many programs that have been instituted in Canada in the past have been, in effect, positive supply management programs. During World War II, for example, subsidies paid per unit of output of pork and other commodities deemed to be desirable by the nation as a whole under the circumstances of war were designed to increase supply when market prices were frozen. In fact, the mechanism of granting either a subsidized or even a guaranteed price for commodities is shown always to force an increase in supply.

More recently, efforts have been made to diversify the mix of agricultural production in the Prairie Provinces, deemphasizing grain and increasing livestock production. This would have two effects: reducing the supply of grain (a problem commodity because of its abundance), and increasing livestock product supply (a problem because of its scarcity relative to demand). The spur employed has also involved a degree of subsidization of inputs (credit) and output prices.

The question of whether positive supply management programs are successful, of course, depends on the goal which they are designed to achieve. The analysis in Chapter 2 shows that the mechanisms of subsidization could not readily improve farm incomes by closing gaps either between farm and nonfarm incomes or disparities of income within the agricultural sector. However, positive supply management programs could be considered useful as adjustment-oriented programs designed to minimize the cost of income maintenance programs, but not as income supportive programs themselves. Such programs could also be useful in forestalling inflationary food price rises, at least in wholesale markets.

Plaunt has accurately pointed out that "there are now, and will be in the future, real constraints imposed [on the adjustment of commercial farms] by the market. Production must be tailored to demand. We cannot [always] adjust demand to suit our production."[1] Whereas the program suggested under the negative supply management section of this chapter would "tailor" production when demand is forecast to be stable or in decline, and where quantities demanded are unlikely to be increased through promotional activity, the programs suggested as positive supply management could tailor production to meet projected increases in demand, either when they occur naturally or are created through promotion.

Part of the need for a policy of positive supply management has already been alluded to: namely, that

---

1. Darrel H. Plaunt, Implications of the Outlook for Adjustment, a paper presented to the Canadian Agricultural Outlook Conference, Ottawa, Nov. 1969.

at certain times the nation has had need of a greater volume of selected agricultural products to serve the national interest than have been offered and has been willing to bear the cost of getting the added supplies. Canada's wartime experience would be an example of this type of action. But the wartime procedures had undesirable side effects to which Canadian agriculture has been forced to accommodate since the wartime policies became part of the Canadian agricultural tradition. Yet, because the nation has new needs in peacetime for agricultural output and selected foods for such national goals as inflation fighting, export growth, and so on, it may be desirable to evolve a set of procedures to stimulate selected production in peacetime, just as it was in wartime. If undesirable side effects could be minimized or eliminated entirely, the principle of using positive supply management could be used to attain new national goals.

In addition there are reasons for programs of positive supply management because of the undesirable influences of uncertainty both on individuals' decision making and on the costs of income-supporting programs. The typical problems of uncertainty for an individual which positive supply management might overcome can be illustrated in a hypothetical example.

If, for example, a farmer learns about a potentially favorable demand situation for a commodity he does not now produce, he would make certain estimates of benefits and costs involved in a change in production. The decision to change his production pattern (that is, tailor his own production to anticipated demand) would depend on whether the benefits outweigh the costs.

The benefits to be considered could include the prospects of a new market with an opportunity to sell a new product, gain a volume of sales, and experience potential growth over a period of time into the future. All these could be quantifiable, although there would be an element of uncertainty in both the price received and the volume of the new commodity he could sell, which would become a discounting element in the calculation. There would also be uncertainty about the price and quantity position in the old commodity depending in part on how many producers actually change production patterns. Hence, the producer's opportunities in other lines would have to be considered, but these are more correctly his opportunity costs. The costs of the change in production pattern would involve, among other things, the actual cost of the changeover. This would include the outlays necessary to purchase new equipment and the losses incurred in scrapping old equipment. Costs associated with changes in management might be minimized because of the availability of appropriate advice through the revitalized information services (Programs 7 and 8); costs associated with the need for land might be minimized because the individual could either buy or lease land from the land agency (Program 10). However, uncertainty would surround the purchase of other inputs depending on how many others decide to take up the new line of production. Also, the individual would consider the uncertainty surrounding his volume of output as a cost because he would not know what volume of production to plan for. This might be reflected in the selection of a production process which would not exhaust all known scale economies even though a more efficient process were known. Hence, for him and society at large, resource use inefficiencies might be introduced.

This situation could be described graphically as in Figure 8.1. This could be a market for a commodity located anywhere. The market need not be necessarily one which producers are now supplying. In fact, it would be a market for a commodity which various producers have not grown before. The initial market situation is shown in Figure 8.1b with demand and supply schedules D_1D_1 and S_1S_1 respectively, giving an equilibrium price P_1 per unit sold and Q_1 units currently being sold. The farmer's share of this would be q_1 as in 8.1a, under conditions set for him by input and output markers. Q_1 in Figure 8.1b is the sum of all q's on the part of individuals. It is not significant for this analysis that the individual under discussion may be producing none of the commodity involved. All this

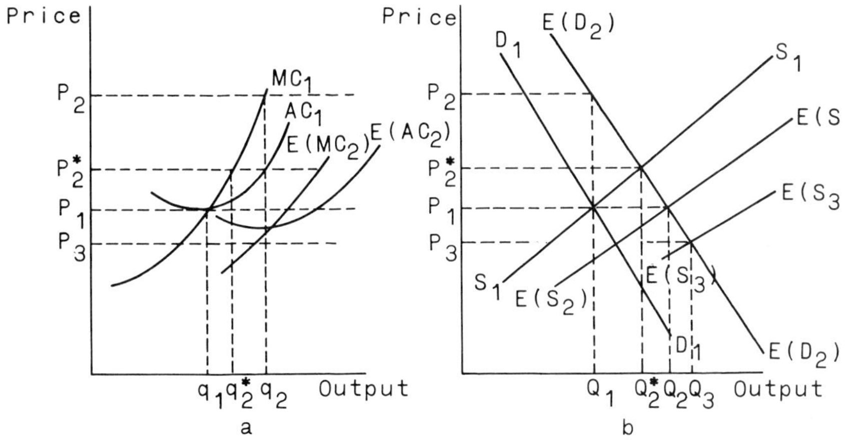

FIG. 8.1. Market and firm equilibrium, with forecast changes in demand.

would imply is that q_1 is very small. We have not associated a scale with the figures. The long-run equilibrium of the firm is represented by q_1, assuming that all abnormal profits have been removed by free entry and exit. The cost curves assume the individual's technology and his personal and financial constraints on production. Now a forecast is made, that in the next (and succeeding) time periods demand will have shifted to D_2D_2 in 8.1b. But, since the forecast would be made with uncertainty, there would be an interval of error around the prediction, but the forecast D_2D_2 could at least be shown as an expected new demand schedule $E(D_2D_2)$.

Initial expectations of the resultant market price might be in the range P_1P_2, provided added supply shifted the market supply schedule to between Q_1 and Q_2. A long-run price expectation might be at P_1, with the volume of sales growing to Q_2, but with the uncertainty of the demand forecast and supply response, price could be lower and volume higher (say at P_3Q_3).

The individual would now be faced with a set of uncertainties separate from those surrounding the forecast. He would have to plan a strategy while not knowing what other individuals are generally planning, but knowing that his own strategy could be frustrated by similar strategies on the part of others.

If he plans to simply expand output with the same facilities, then he could easily miss his income-maximizing point (by producing at q_2 when P_2^* was realized for example, or at q_2^* if a price below P_2^* emerges). If he decides to change scale, the discounted future costs might be seriously misjudged relative to actual realized returns. The new cost structure if new investment occurs [$E(MC_2)$ and $E(AC_2)$] might be such as to force a shutdown if others also increase supply and aggregate supply forces a market price of P_3. [$E(MC_2)$ and $E(AC_2)$ are drawn to imply increasing economies of scale.] These and other uncertainties would add to the cost of a changeover, or of commencing a new operation.

The policy of positive supply management would be justified, if only to minimize the costs of such uncertainty to individuals. But if programs for income support were initiated, positive supply management could also help minimize government outlays.

The programs in Chapter 5, especially Program 2, were suggested as an attempt to stabilize incomes at some "historic" mean for a farm family, so that farm income could be effectively shielded from the instabilities of agricultural production. They were also designed so that adjustment could proceed while still ensuring a minimum living level. Part of the adjustment process would involve the switching of enterprises as changes in demand made themselves felt. If there were no effective means of forecasting and then directing various farmers into new production lines, the costs of the income stabilization and maintenance programs could be greater than if such positive supply management programs existed. If the individual is more or less insured against all uncertainty of income by Program 2, society at large would have to bear the cost. Thus, the lower the variance in prices, the smaller the cost of public programs would be.

In response to this a policy concerning positive supply management would be justified as a means of facilitating least-cost, ongoing adjustment. But because for some producers there would be real benefits in excess of the costs they would have to bear, derived from changing production patterns, a blanket program of paying subsidies per unit of output would not be necessary. The question then becomes one of discovering an appropriate mechanism which can be used under control, which will still permit economic efficiency in production, allow for private goal attainment, and be consistent with the other policies of adjustment within agriculture.

It is completely obvious that if the outlook—the forecast—is not accurate the rest of the policy process is of little use in giving a positive result to society. This has been pointed out elsewhere, particularly in the context of quantitative policy making and planning.[2] Forecasts tend to minimize the costs of general uncertainty; better forecasts reduce costs further. It is therefore incumbent on the forecaster to use the best causal economic reasoning and statistical techniques available when preparing forecasts, particularly when the forecaster is in a governmental directing agency, and in a place of prominence. But this is an area in which new programs can serve little useful purpose. Time constraints on researchers, data limitations, the cost of error in relation to the cost of reducing the error, all impose constraints on the attainment of perfect forecasts. Even so, an appropriate policy mechanism could minimize the costs of poor forecasts for farmers and for the government, which would have undertaken to support the living levels of the farmer.

Some of the reasons for vertical integration occurring rapidly in some industries (notably the poultry industry) appear to offer a clue to the appropriate mechanism. The contracting arrangement between produc-

---

2. See, for example, Henri Theil, Applied Economic Forecasting (Amsterdam: North Holland Publ. Co., 1966).

ers and wholesale buyers has been in part a response to uncertainty in production and outlook for sales. If the amount to be produced and delivered over a period of three or four production cycles could be specified, the operator could be specified and could act to maximize net income and realize savings that would not occur if he were forced to maximize separately in each of three or four successive periods. This principle has been applied in economic development planning and plant management, and has been suggested in agricultural production economic studies.

A program operated by the government could attain similar results for farmers in general.

Program 13: Increasing Output of Specific Commodities in Specific Regions without Government Payments

Purpose. This program would have the effect of removing two of the three main causes of uncertainty encountered by farmers as they either expand production or embark on new enterprises: the uncertainty of their discounted future costs relative to expected price, and the uncertainty of the market price itself. (The third uncertainty, that of outlook information itself, would be considered a public cost and would be underwritten in Program 2.)

Elements of the Program. Government or the agency designated as responsible for positive supply management would forecast new demand, which would arise either through natural or promotional forces. With this in hand, the agency would estimate a range of prices, for example, P_1P_2 in Figure 8.1b, which could result in free market actions, and decide upon one which they believe represents a fair trade-off between consumers' and farmers' interests. (If farmers could prevent free entry and regulate the supply of produce offered, they would maximize their benefits by producing at Q_1P_2. Consumers would gain most if producers were forced to supply Q_2.) The target price would be between P_1 and P_2—probably between P_1 and P_2^*, which represents the price that would result if only established producers in established enterprises sold more output. The desired increment in output would then be given.

Calculations based on technical information would show a size of enterprise and a volume of output under given input prices and technology and the target output price which would constitute a minimum profit contract lot. Minimum profit would be judged to include a fair return to entrepreneurship after labor and capital costs are covered. The agency could estimate the number of contract lots that would be sufficient to meet the projected demand increase. These would be offered to farmers on a bid basis. Farmers would have an opportunity to bid for a contract lot by indicating the price they would be willing to accept per unit of output if the contract were for a specific output at a specific price in each of five years, for example. The contracts would be let first to the bidders willing to accept the lowest price, then to the next, and so on. The government agency would collect the product (or at least arrange shipment), pay the farmer the price he bid, and resell the output in the market involved.

Indeed, if an agreement between the government and a producer marketing board could be arranged, government could merely withdraw and be only a financial backer, not an operator of the scheme. If government errs and lets out too many contracts, it would have to hold the excess and not permit it to affect the market prices, for the sake of those who are not under contract and have to take the market price. If government errs by contracting for too little, it would simply let out another contract to pick up the slack.

Obviously, this scheme would not apply to all commodities in all regions of the country. Where markets are already developed and working, or where chronic surpluses occur, this program is not applicable. But where markets are not developed—in commodities and regions where it could be economically feasible for them if only some certainty and more perfect knowledge could be obtained—this program has a role. For example, it could be used in the Maritime Provinces to create a hog industry or barley production. In this area hog production could be economically sound, as could barley production, but local uncertainty seems to prevent it.[3]

If it were deemed desirable to assist producers in specific income classes (for example, those in the $5,000 to $10,000 class and under forty-five years of age), the program could favor their bids.

Costs. The program would have minimal costs, since the government would not generally pay out more, or less, than it received in the markets of final sale. If the government undertook to underwrite the program financially but leave operations to producer marketing boards, even administrative costs would be minimized. The program, in effect, is an attempt to remove some of the expense of adjustment by removing uncertainty.

Termination. This program would not have to proceed perpetually for any given product, for once producers have commenced production under the encouragement of a five-year certainty contract, they would be in a position to begin developing and servicing their market directly. Government would not necessarily have to let a second set of contracts.

Special management advice in this regard would help terminate government's role. If the producer marketing board assumes the duties associated with positive supply management, government would only have to insure that the board is not preventing reasonable free entry.

The program would spur the production of socially desired commodities for whatever goal government held to be important. Regional development, inflation control, export stimulation—all could be served by such a program. More significant, however, would be the feature which makes the program selective. It would be a program of controlled output stimulation, not a blanket invitation to farmers to produce at their own risk, as was the wartime policy. In this way, no undesirable side effects would be felt.

---

3. See Acres Research and Planning, "Problems, Policies and Prospects for the Feedgrain-Livestock Economy," report to the Federal Task Force on Agriculture, 1969, vol. 1, table 12, and vol. 4, pp. 68 ff. Available at the Canadian Dept. of Agr. Library, Ottawa.

NEW PROGRAMS TO IMPLEMENT NEGATIVE SUPPLY MANAGEMENT

The need for supply management to encourage the production of specific commodities in specific times and places might be considered less pressing when compared to the more urgent policy need to overcome problems of general oversupply in most agricultural commodities. Oversupply, of course, means a supply in excess of given or expected demands at product prices which would be adequate to yield a return to resources in agriculture comparable to those earned in the nonfarm sector.

To date the public has attempted to mitigate the effects of general oversupply by employing policy mechanisms such as paying subsidies on output (price support) or restricting supply either directly (delivery quotas) or indirectly (input quotas). But these mechanisms have not generally permitted the farm sector to retain many of the income benefits sought; in fact, the sector has lost welfare relative even to its former position.

The analysis in Chapter 2 would suggest that as an alternative to the use of supply management mechanisms to achieve some income goal (which it might be able to do), the mechanisms could be better used to stabilize prices and incomes and minimize the cost of the direct income support programs outlined in Chapter 5. Since most of the cost of the income support programs outlined would be associated with oversupply and low prices, supplemental negative supply management programs would provide a vital service. But to permit ongoing adjustment, negative supply management would need to be free of quotas.

<u>Elements of Policy</u>. The desirable elements of a negative supply management program could be outlined in a more or less abstract discussion of a policy mechanism which features supply restraint and price stabilization and improvement. But in contrast to present farm programs which use marketing quotas (the mandatory imposition of producer quotas) and proposed programs to withdraw land from production, such as the LIFT Program of 1970, the mechanism can attain the same level of supply control and price improvement with neither

government payments nor imposed marketing quotas.[4] The method suggested below would place no restraints on a farmer's freedom of choice in matters pertinent to least-cost production. Under present programs, all producers of the commodity under a marketing board's control are forced to limit their production by at least an equal proportional—if not absolute—amount, regardless of their income benefit. (See Chap. 2 on quota assigment.) The farmer's willingness to cooperate in controlling supply in this program would be proportional to what he sees as his gain in profits. Finally, even with all these positive features which present programs lack, the mechanism would yield the same effects on the levels of food prices and progressiveness of food costs relative to income as does any other program which results in the same level of supply control and price improvement.

With a marketing board arrangement, the farmer could be viewed as being a landlord and the board essentially a tenant. The board takes a varying amount of produce, or the product of a varying number of acres, and sells it, returning to the farmer a payment as "rent." This arrangement would describe the actions of the Canada Wheat Board, which allocates acreage quota by agreeing to sell products grown on certain acres which it in effect rents. The proposed mechanism would in a sense reverse the situation—the board or agency serving implicitly as "the landlord" and the farmer as a "tenant." However, the board or agency would not become the owner of the land, but only receive a share of output. In contrast to the present system wherein the board, as tenant, pays a cash rent to the farmer, as landlord, the farmer would, as tenant equivalent, but still the owner and independent decision maker, pay a rent in kind to the agency.

The use of this terminology is intended to indicate only that the proposed mechanism uses basic economics, known for some time in the field of tenant-landlord relationships, and relies upon the known effects of share-renting with respect to production decisions, as

4. This mechanism is also discussed in E. O. Heady, Tax in Kind to Reduce Supply, Am. J. Ag. Econ. 53(Aug. 1971): 441-47.

opposed to cash-renting—not that new ownership patterns should be enforced.[5] Basically, farmers paying rent in kind should offer smaller supplies than cash renters. If the recipient of the rent in kind is the marketing board, the result should be that prices could be stabilized by varying the terms of the "rental agreement." But this would be accomplished at no cost to the government. The agency might use its "rent" for instance, for international food aid donations, or simply bury it, with the acquisition costs of the commodities being zero, but having the effect of reducing domestic supply and raising prices and income; or it could place its share of output on the domestic market again. In either case, total marketed supply would still be decreased, as compared to the situation in which there was no program.

Model of the Mechanism. To illustrate and maintain simplicity, the following model deals with a single commodity and a single agricultural resource to reflect production and cost relationships. (The results would be the same regardless of the algebraic relationships employed as long as we assume a price elasticity of demand less than unity, which is the case of basic agricultural commodities in any event, and a supply elasticity greater than zero, also true for agriculture.) The numerical parameters used to provide a degree of specificity slightly overstate the conditions surrounding agriculture but are used for purposes of emphasis. They would at least qualitatively describe the farm economy.

Let the demand function be Equation 8.1 where

$$P = \beta Q_d^{-2} \tag{8.1}$$

$$Q_p = \alpha X^{0.5} \tag{8.2}$$

The price elasticity of demand is -0.5, β reflects income, population, and consumer preference components

5. See Earl O. Heady, Economics of Agricultural Production and Resource Use (New York: Prentice-Hall, 1952), especially Chap. 20 and 21.

of demand, while P and Q_d are respectively the market price and quantity variables. We assume n "representative" farms make up the producing sector. Each farm has a fixed component of production denoted as α/n reflecting fixed inputs of several resources and their transformation coefficients. When all farms have perfect knowledge and maximize profits relative to production restraints, prices, and technical coefficients, the aggregate production function of the producing sector is Equation 8.2 where Q_p is output, and X is a variable resource or a collection of variable inputs used in a given mix. Under these normative assumptions, the sector's total cost function would be Equation 8.3, and its marginal cost function would be Equation 8.4, where P_x is the price of output.

$$TC = \alpha^{-2} P_x Q_p^2 \qquad (8.3)$$

$$MC = 2\alpha^{-2} P_x Q_p \qquad (8.4)$$

Equating marginal cost to price, the commodity supply function would be

$$Q_s = 0.5\alpha^2 P P_x^{-1} \qquad (8.5)$$

In equilibrium, the demand function in Equation 8.1 and the supply function in Equation 8.5 are equated and generate equilibrium market price and quantity, farm revenue, total costs, and net revenue. These are tabulated in Table 8.1. So computed, the quantities reflect the situation (as denoted by the subscript 1) before any policy is implemented.

Suppose now that farmers, in the role of tenants, paying for the right to produce a certain crop, pay their rent in kind, and that it amounts to a flat rate of 20 percent of their total output. Further, assume that the agency (the marketing board) does not dispose of its share in the market, but rather offers it as free food aid to a developing nation.

Basic demand and production functions would remain

Table 8.1. Market Solution with Negative Supply Control under Alternate Disposal Systems

Item	Original Solution	Solution without Board Resale in Market	Solution with Board Resale in Market
Market price, P_y	$P_1 = 2^{2/3}\alpha^{-4/3}\beta^{1/3}P_x^{2/3}$	$P_2 = 1.25^{4/3}P_1$	$P_3 = 1.25^{2/3}P_1$
Market quantity, Q	$Q_1 = 2^{-1/3}\alpha^{2/3}\beta^{1/3}P_x^{-1/3}$	$Q_2 = 0.8^{2/3}Q_1$	$Q_3 = 0.8^{1/3}Q_1$
Total farm revenue, $TR = P_y \cdot Q$	$TR_1 = 2^{1/3}\alpha^{-2/3}\beta^{2/3}P_x^{1/3}$	$TR_2 = 0.8^{-2/3}TR_1$	$TR_3 = 1.25^{1/3}TR_1$
Total farm costs, $TC = X \cdot P_x$	$TC_1 = 2^{-2/3}\alpha^{-2/3}\beta^{2/3}P_x^{1/3}$	$TC_2 = 1.25^{2/3}TC_1$	$TC_3 = 1.25^{-2/3}TC_1$
Net farm revenue, NR = TR − TC	$\pi_1 = (2^{1/3} - 2^{-2/3})\alpha^{-2/3}\beta^{2/3}P_x^{1/3}$	$\pi_2 = 1.25^{2/3}\pi_1$*	$\pi_3 = 1.28\pi_1$†

*$\pi_2 = [(1.25^{2/3})(2^{1/3}) - (1.25^{2/3})(2^{-2/3})]\alpha^{-2/3}\beta^{2/3}P_x^{1/3}$

†$\pi_3 = [(1.25^{1/3})(2^{1/3}) - (0.8^{2/3})(2^{-2/3})]\alpha^{-2/3}\beta^{2/3}P_x^{1/3}$

the same as in Equations 8.1 and 8.2; but with 20 percent of output going as rent in kind, realized farm share would be

$$Q_p = (0.8)\alpha X^{0.5} \quad (8.6)$$

(expressed as a quantity, not the function as in Equation 8.2). Thus the operative input demand function would be

$$X' = (1.25)^2\alpha^{-2}Q_p^{\ 2} \quad (8.7)$$

and new total cost and aggregate supply functions would be

$$TC' = (1.25)^2\alpha^{-2}P_xQ_p^{\ 2} \quad (8.8)$$

and

$$Q_s' = (0.5)(1.25)^{-2}\alpha^2 PP_x^{\ -1} \quad (8.9)$$

Q_s' would be the supply representing farmers' offerings at different money commodity prices P and input prices P_x. The backward shift in the supply function relative to Equation 8.5 would be due to the farmers' reassessment of their optimal production decisions after paying rent in kind rather than a money rent, which would have been a part of P_x. This is a standard conclusion of landlord-tenant economics. In essence, when the farmer pays rent in kind, he pays a progressive tax (the more he produces, the more in absolute terms he pays the landlord), regardless of the flat rate feature. This is an incentive to him to reconsider his optimal production point. If he pays rent as a fixed money sum per acre, the rent would be part of fixed costs, a cost incurred regardless of the level of production, and would then not influence the decision to produce.

The potency of the "variable rent" element in the operation of this mechanism would make it work well in keeping total supply in check. If money rents were paid progressively with output, they would also become a variable cost of production and result in a similar retardation of output flows. This aspect is outlined below.

Now with supply function as in Equation 8.9 and demand in Equation 8.1, a new market equilibrium would result. The corresponding commodity price, supply quantity, farm revenue, total farm costs, and net profits (subscripted 2) are given in Table 8.1 in terms of the original solution.

The individual farmer is not restrained in any manner, in that he can produce to his heart's content (i.e., so that profit is maximized by equating marginal cost with market price, as under the absence of a program). Yet the system would generate a marked improvement in price ($P_2 = 1.25^{4/3}P_1$), total market revenue ($TR_2 = 1.25^{2/3}TR_1$), and profit ($\pi_2 = 1.25^{2/3}\pi_1$). Marketed supply is reduced ($Q_2 = 0.8^{2/3}Q_1$). Total costs increase ($TC_2 = 1.25^{2/3}TC_1$) since the total output, including the agency's share which is not marketed, now is greater than the original equilibrium output, Q_1. The share marketed by farmers is Q_2, but since the agency receives an amount equal to $0.25Q_2$, total produced output is actually $1.25Q_2$ (with $0.25Q_2$ held from the market) which is an amount larger than Q_1 (i.e., total output of $1.25Q_2 = 1.25^{1/3}Q_1$). Yet the large increase in price and total revenue, from P_1 to $1.25^{4/3}P_1$ and TR_1 to $1.25^{2/3}TR_1$ respectively, is not accompanied by costs which reduce net revenue. Not only would the system increase equilibrium price, market revenue, and net profit, but also it would provide a food fund of $0.25Q_1$, which could be used as international aid or for other humanitarian causes at no acquisition cost to government.

But suppose that world food supplies increase and hunger decreases on its own so that shipments of food from North America are not needed, or that the Canadian population has values which prevent the board from actually destroying a share of food produced. Will the system still work?

It would, but with a somewhat muted impact (a preset target impact could be attained by having a larger share go to the board). To illustrate, suppose that the agency takes a 0.2 share of total output as rent in kind, but places it on the domestic market. Since the sharing arrangement increases marginal costs to farmers of their own share, it still reduces supply and improves price and income when compared with the situation before any such program existed.

The total cost function relative to their 0.8 share for farmers under this policy construct would be the same as Equation 8.2. But by adding the government's share (20 percent of the total or a 0.25 proportion of the farmer's share) to the market, the total supply function would be Equation 8.10. With demand remaining as Equation 8.1 and with total market supply in Equation 8.10 equated to demand, a third market solution would prevail. The magnitudes (subscripted 3) are given in Table 8.1.

$$Q_s'' = (1.25^{-1})(0.5)\alpha^2 PP_x^{-1} \tag{8.10}$$

The total revenue is that forthcoming from the sale of the 0.8 share of farmers' and 0.2 share of government output. Hence, this total revenue is realized by farmers only if the government transfers its 0.2 share of total revenue back to farmers. The net farm profit expressed as π_3 supposes this to be the case. If this were not the case, government or the agency would be taxing the farm commodity by its resale of the commodity. One cannot imagine this as a politically feasible action, particularly when the transfer could be made as part of the programs outlined in Chapters 6 and 7.

The market price, P_3, is greater under this system than with "no program," P_1. Of course, it is lower than the price, P_2, when the government disposes of its share in nonmarket channels. If the agency also put its share on the market, the equilibrium market supply of Q_3 would be smaller than the market supply in the absence of a program. The higher marginal costs to the farmer for his share would damp his production as compared to "no program." Total costs would be lower and net profit larger, even with the agency marketing its share domestically, than in the absence of a program. Further, π_3 exceeds π_1. In the expression for π_3, the multiplier 1.25 is larger and the multiplier $0.8^{2/3}$ is smaller than the implied multipliers of unity in the expression for π_1. Accordingly, π_3 is greater than π_1.

As compared to "no program," farmers would have higher prices, revenue, and profit because the marginal costs of obtaining their own share of output would be higher and the marketed supply less. The government would make no payments to farmers to reduce supply (the transfer of revenue cannot be considered a cost); the "tenure arrangement" would choke down supply and cause price and net income to increase under the inelastic demand.

A comparison of the case where the agency markets its share of the product domestically, rather than insulating it from the market, would show that total net farm income would be higher when the agency actively sells domestically. That is,

$$\pi_3 > \pi_2 > \pi_1$$

The full comparison is given in Table 8.2.

The effect of the policy mechanism in terms of the expressions used here would also depend on the share diverted to the board. Table 8.2 shows price, output, revenue, and net profit levels for the 20 percent share used in the above calculations for a 10 percent share. Based on the algebraic forms and numerical coefficients of Equations 8.1 and 8.2, the price increase when the agency takes a 10 percent share and

Table 8.2. Price, Output Revenue, and Net Profit Levels under Two Share Magnitudes

Policy Alternative	Equilibrium Price with Government Share of 0.2	0.1	Equilibrium Output with Government Share of[a] 0.2	0.1	Total Revenue with Government Share of[b] 0.2	0.1	Net Profit with Government Share of 0.2	0.1
No program	P_1	P_1	Q_1	Q_1	TR_1	TR_1	π_1	π_1
Government ships share[a]	$P_2 = 1.35P_1$	$P_2 = 1.15P_1$	$Q_2 = 0.86Q_1$	$Q_2 = 0.93Q_1$	$TR_2 = 1.16TR_1$	$TR_2 = 1.07TR_1$	$\pi_2 = 1.16\pi_1$	$\pi_2 = 1.07\pi_1$
Government markets share	$P_3 = 1.16P_1$	$P_3 = 1.07P_1$	$Q_3 = 0.93Q_1$	$Q_3 = 0.97Q_1$	$TR_3 = 1.08TR_1$	$TR_3 = 1.04TR_1$	$\pi_3 = 1.28\pi_1$	$\pi_3 = 1.14\pi_1$
	$= 0.85P_2$	$= 0.03P_2$	$= 1.08Q_2$	$= 1.04Q_2$	$= 0.93TR_2$	$= 0.97TR_2$	$= 1.10\pi_2$	$= 1.07\pi_2$

[a]When the government takes a share but does not market it, total output is actually $1.25Q_2$ (where Q_2 is the marketed quantity). For a 0.2 share, total output then is $1.08Q_1$ while for a 0.1 share it is $1.16Q_1$.

[b]If the production elasticity in Equation 8.2 in the text were unity, and the elasticity of supply were infinite (an unlikely case for agriculture in aggregate), the price, output, and revenue quantities where the government gets a 0.2 share of total output and "ships" it would be $P_1 = 1.25P_1$, $Q_2 = 0.89Q_1$, and $TR_2 = 1.12TR_1$. However, P_3 and TR_3 would be smaller than P_1 and TR_1.

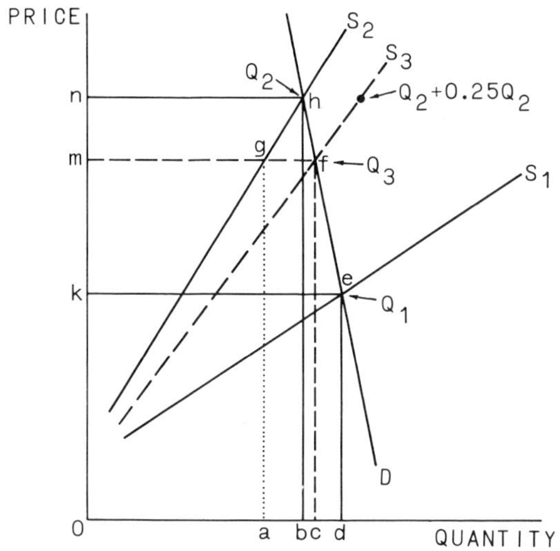

FIG. 8.2. Effects on price, supply, and market revenue.

holds it from the market is only about half that when the share is 20 percent. For general increments in price, revenue and profit are lower under a 10 percent share than under a 20 percent share. Output also is greater. For example, when the government markets its share, output is 93 percent of the original output under a 20 percent share, but 96 percent of original output under a 10 percent share.

While not all these quantities can be included in a simple geometric presentation, the general effect of the mechanism on price, market revenue, and supply quantity might be summarized as in Figure 8.2. The demand function D indicates a price elasticity less than unity. (The diagram is not intended to reflect the magnitudes or functions in the algebraic example.) Under the conditions of "no program," the supply function would be S_1 and market revenue would be Odek. With the farmers' marketing board taking the implied share of the output and withholding it from the domestic market, supply would decline to S_2 and market revenue would be Obhn, an amount considerably greater than Odek. Supply function S_2 denotes only the quantity marketed by farmers. It does not represent total production at each price. Total output at each price is $1.25S_2$ since farmers would retain a 0.8 share and the agency would receive a 0.2 share of total production. However, when the agency places its share on the market, total domestic market supply (total production in this case) then becomes S_3 and total revenue is Ocfm. (The function of total output—$1.25S_2$ including the government's share, since S_2 represents only the 0.8 portion marketed by farmers—is identical with the function S_3, which denotes total output under the situation.) Since the product share to the farmers' board is 0.2, the agency share of total revenue is acfg and the farmers' share is Oagm. If the agency returns its share to farmers, the total revenue of farmers becomes Ocfm, an amount larger than the original revenue of Odek.

Figure 8.2 also summarizes the relative magnitudes of output explained in the algebraic presentation. The quantity Q_1 expresses equilibrium market output under P_1. The quantity Q_2 is in the 0.8 proportion of total output marketed by farmers when the agency takes its share off the domestic market. (Total output is $1.25Q_2$, with the agency removing a 0.2 share of this from the market.) However, when the agency also markets its 0.2 share, the equilibrium total output is Q_3. Hence, $1.25Q_2$ is greater than both Q_1 and Q_3.

This mechanism would provide a rather unique policy instrument for reducing supply, increasing prices and income, and acquiring a food fund for international aid at zero farm cost to the government and without imposition of marketing quotas. Of course, in any actual implementation the government would have handling and transport costs for its share exported as aid or used to alleviate domestic hunger. But it has had these costs in all previous programs. If it markets its share domestically, it would have related handling costs. But because of the smaller output than under "no program" these costs also would be lower and the total net revenue which could be returned to farmers would still increase.

Alternate Model of the Mechanism. The analysis to this point has been somewhat abstract. But under real world conditions one would expect farmers to use less fertilizer and other production inputs if a share of their output is paid to an agency without the agency paying a proportionate share of costs. The extent to which output would be damped or the share required to restrain output and stabilize prices at particular levels could not be specified for Canada without statistical analysis. But lack of quantitative knowledge has always prevailed as various policy elements were initiated in the past. Under a policy mechanism such as the one presented, experimentation through implementation would probably be required to generate data for analysis.

Intuitively it would seem to be a less costly alternative when using the principles involved in the preceding discussion to actually implement the programs using a system of progressive cash "fee payments," or what would amount to a set of progressive taxes imposed by the board for the stabilization of product prices and incomes. To the extent that boards using the instrument were producer-elected boards, or politically responsive, producers would then be effectively taxing themselves. Using progressive cash payments in lieu of payments in kind, the many problems associated with storage, commodity movements, and resale would be avoided.

The essential logic of the producer board's levying a progressive "tax" on its producers would closely parallel that given above. A simple model would illustrate the mechanism and its effects in reducing output and increasing farm income potential. (While a specific algebraic formulation is used because of its ease of manipulation, the results would be generally true for any set of commodities with price elasticities of demand less than 1.0.)

Assume an industry production function as in Equation 8.11 and a demand function as in Equation 8.12:

$$Q_p = \alpha X^b \tag{8.11}$$

$$Q_d = \delta P^{-e} \tag{8.12}$$

As in Equation 8.2 all variable inputs are subsumed in index form in X (and all short-run fixed inputs in α), and P is price (marginal revenue) per unit of output. The conclusions which follow would apply to all values of e, the price elasticity, $0 < e < 1.0$.

From the production function, input requirements are as in Equation 8.13, total costs are given in Equation 8.14, and marginal costs are derived as in Equation 8.15, where P_x is the price of inputs.

$$X = \alpha^{-1/b} Q_p^{1/b} \tag{8.13}$$

$$TC = P_x X = \alpha^{-1/b} Q^{1/b} P_x \tag{8.14}$$

$$MC = (1/b) \cdot \alpha^{-1/b} P_x Q_p^{(1/b-1)} = b^{-1} \alpha^{-1/b} P_x Q_p^{(1-b)/b} \tag{8.15}$$

Assuming virtually perfect competition and farmer objectives of profit maximization, the supply function becomes

$$Q_s = (b\alpha^{1/b} P P_x^{-1})^{b/(1-b)} \tag{8.16}$$

In market equilibrium, demand equals supply, hence $Q_s = Q_d$. The equilibrium price P_1, quantity Q_1, total revenue TR_1, total cost TC_1, and net revenue π_1 derived from the above relationship are given in Table 8.3.

Thus, farmers in aggregate would earn TR_1 which comes from their direct sales of output in domestic markets. π_1 is the profit derived from market operations and indicates the level of welfare of farmers.

Now let farmers tax themselves through the board which they may control so that they receive, effec-

Table 8.3. Market Solution with Negative Supply Management Using Money Tax

Item	Original Solution	Solution with Tax of $(1-r)$ per Unit
Market price, P_y	$P_1 = b^{-b/s} \alpha^{-1/s} \delta^{(1-b)/s} P_x^{b/s}$*	$P_2 = r^{-b/s} P_1$
Market quantity, Q	$Q_1 = b^{be/s} \alpha^{e/s} \delta^{b/s} P_x^{-be/s}$	$Q_2 = r^{be/s} Q_1$
Total farm revenue, $TR = P_y \cdot Q$	$TR_1 = b^{b(e-1)/s} \alpha^{(e-1)/s} \delta^{1/s} P_x^{b(1-e)/s}$	$TR_2 = r^{b(e-1)/s} TR_1$
Total farm costs, $TC = X \cdot P_x$	$TC_1 = b^{e/s} \alpha^{(e-s)/sb} \delta^{1/s} P_x^{(s-e)/s}$†	$TC_2 = r^{e/s} TC_1$
Net farm revenue	$\pi_1 = [b^{b(e-1)/s} - b^{e/s}] \alpha^{(e-1)/s} \delta^{1/s} P_x^{b(1-e)/s}$	$\pi_2 = r^{b(e-s)/s} [(1-rb)/(1-b)] \pi_1$‡
$NR = TR - TC$	$= (1-b) b^{b(e-1)/s} \alpha^{(e-1)/s} \delta^{1/s} P_x^{b(1-e)/s}$	

*$s = (b + e - eb)$

†$(e-1)/s = (e-s)/sb$ and $b(1-e)/s = (s-e)/s$

‡$\pi_1 = [(br)^{b(e-1)/s} - (br)^{e/s}] \alpha^{(e-1)/s} \delta^{1/s} P_x^{(s-e)/s}$

tively, r•P as a price per unit of output ($0 < r < 1$). In the example the tax rate is a constant, regardless of the level of output for simplicity. Whatever conclusions hold in this case would certainly hold if r is progressive with output levels. This is similar to the case described earlier which dealt with tax in kind.

The board receives (1−r)P per unit sold as its share, and the normative supply function would be as shown in Equation 8.17. The quantity offered for the prevailing equilibrium market price would be reduced by r proportion

$$Q_s' = [b \cdot \alpha^{1/b} P_x^{-1} (r \cdot P)] \exp(b/1-b) \quad (8.17)$$

relative to the original supply, Equation 8.16, since, at the same levels of average and marginal cost, effective marginal revenue to the farmer would decline. Or, with the tax collected prior to production as outlined later, the quantity (1−r)P could be considered an addition to average, and marginal, cost since the farmer would have to pay the amount of tax to his board for the "right" to produce.

A new market equilibrium would occur when $Q_s' = Q_d$ at the new price, quantity, and other market-determined magnitudes (subscripted 2) described in Table 8.3 in terms of the original solution.

Thus the paradoxical situation would again exist in which farmers, willing to accept lower per unit returns for output, increase the potential profit to the sector. This is a qualitatively different result than could be expected with "normal" marketing board operations, in which boards try to improve profits by reducing output offered for sale and assigning production or delivery quotas to farmers. In the case illustrated here, production would seek its own level in line with profit-maximizing principles (it is not controlled directly as in a quota system). Rather, output and income would be controlled through the board's manipulation of r. When $r = 1$, $(1-r) = 0$ and $\pi_2 = \pi_1$; that is, when farmers pay no fees or taxes to the board, there is no change in the sector's profit. Manipulating r downward would have the effect of progressively raising π. See Table 8.4 for any given production or demand situation. (The optimal level of r could be shown to be 0, using differential calculus. This would imply that farmers would gain the most by receiving no income direct from private market sales, and receiving all income as payments from the board.)

The total revenue and profit magnitudes given in Table 8.3, TR_1 and π_2, are earned by the sector, and farmers would receive only part of these funds directly from the sale of produce. If TR_F and π_F are the total revenue and profits earned by farmers directly from the sale of products, then

$$TR_F = r \cdot TR_2 = r^{e/s} TR_1 \tag{8.18}$$

$$\pi_F = TR_F - TC_2 = r^{e/s} \pi_1 \tag{8.19}$$

Table 8.4. Estimated Growth in Profits from Supply Management by Taxing the Product Price

	Value of r			
Value of b	0.2	0.4	0.6	0.8
		e = 0.8		
0.4	1.79	1.53	1.33	1.16
0.6	2.71	2.15	1.71	1.34
0.8	5.50	3.94	2.83	1.87
		e = 0.4		
0.4	2.81	1.97	1.53	1.14
0.6	4.71	2.93	2.03	1.44
0.8	10.08	5.61	3.42	2.03
		e = 0.2		
0.4	4.12	2.46	1.53	1.30
0.6	6.84	3.63	2.29	1.52
0.8	14.32	6.83	3.85	2.12

Note: Growth multiple is π_2/π_1 as described in the text, and the actual estimate is given by

$$\{r \cdot \exp\,[b(e - 1)/(b + e - eb)]\} \cdot \{(1 - rb)/(1 - b)\}$$

where $Q_p = \alpha X^b$ and $Q_d = \delta P^{-e}$.

Clearly, farmers would be receiving less revenue from the market and making smaller profits from direct farming operations under the scheme, because they would be sharing receipts with the board, while the board pays more of the expenses of farming. The board's share of the total revenue TR_B and profit π_B would be respectively

$$TR_B = TR_2 - TR_F = (1-r)r^{b(e-1)/s}TR_1 \quad (8.20)$$

$$\pi_B = \pi_2 - \pi_F = (1-b)^{-1}(1-r)r^{b(e-1)/s}\pi_1 \quad (8.21)$$

For farmers to be better off with the operation of the mechanism than without it, that is, for $\pi_F \geqq \pi_1$, the board would have to administer its share of the revenue in a way that (1) it transfers enough back to farmers so that their previous level of welfare (for which π_1 was a proxy) is maintained, and (2) it does this so that the essential character of the policy is maintained. The board would have to decide on levels of the tax rate $1-r$, or the level of the farmer's direct dependence on the market for his income r, rather than on board transfers. As indicated in Table 8.4 the optimal rate would probably be $r = 0$. But farmers may be reluctant to surrender their complete independence, even if it is for their own financial good.

The degree to which producers would be willing to form such a strong bond with the board controlling their product would limit the degree to which producers are able to gain from such a program as suggested here. If producers recognize that they could enjoy real income stability as a result of Program 2, regardless of the actions of the board in varying the price it pays or the quantity it accepts from producers to sell, farmer acceptance of the ideas involved would probably grow. But this acceptance is not subject to legislation or regulation. The "best" size of r and $1-r$ is that which would emerge after debate and compromise reveal the subjective trade-offs made by farmers generally between higher income and greater independence from a cooperative board.

It is relatively simple to demonstrate that the board's share, TR_B or π_B, would be large enough to restore farmer welfare to its preprogram level and still leave a surplus in the board's treasury for administration, promotional activity, conference organization, political contribution, and so on. Welfare would be maintained if the board transfers back to farmers an amount y such that $\pi_1 = \pi_F + y$. The board will have a surplus if $\pi_B - y > 0$, or if (substituting for y_B and for y)

$$[(1-b)^{-1}(1-r)r^{b(e-1)/s}\pi_1] - [\pi_1 - r^{e/s}\pi_1] > 0 \tag{8.22}$$

By factoring, Equation 8.22 is equivalent to

$$\pi_1[(1-b)^{-1}r^{b(e-1)/s} - (1-b)^{-1}r^{e/s} - 1 + r^{e/s}] > 0 \tag{8.23}$$

which, since $\pi_1 > 0$, is true if

$$(1-b)^{-1}r^{b(e-1)/s} - b(1-b)^{-1}r^{e/s} > 1 \tag{8.24}$$

or if

$$(1-b)^{-1} - [(b/(1-b)]r > r^{b(1-e)/s} \tag{8.25}$$

(multiplying through by $r^{b(1-1)/s}$, which is greater than 0), or if

$$(1-rb)/(1-b) > r^{b(1-e)/s} \tag{8.26}$$

or if

$$(1-rb) > r^{b(1-e)/s} - br^{b(1-e)/s} \tag{8.27}$$

But since $1 > r^{b(1-e)/s}$, and $r^{b(1-e)/s} > r$, so that $br^{b(1-e)/s} > br$, then $(1-rb)$ is in fact greater than $[r^{b(1-e)/s} - br^{b(1-e)/s}]$; the board would always be able to ensure that farmers would not lose their farmer welfare position, and could in addition provide services for the farmers under the board's authority.

The method of effecting the transfer so that the essential logic of the policy is not invalidated would pose a more serious problem. Recalling that the positive income benefits were possible because the tax (1—r) was paid as an expense per unit, with the effect of shifting the entire offer curve backward, suggests that transferring wealth back to farmers in any manner which can be interpreted as a return per unit of output would completely negate the effects of the taxing method. The effects of transferring wealth to farmers in a manner fully and positively correlated with output have been recognized for years, in the criticism that per unit subsidies increase the supply price and shift the entire supply curve outward. This could be observed in the analysis of output price subsidies given in Chapter 2.

However, there would still be many options open to the board for transferring wealth. First, the board could pay for essentially fixed costs like management advice, or help individual needy farmers with living allowances, apart from their individual incomes through sales in the manner of family equalization payments. Other fraternal ventures could be undertaken on behalf of all producers such as scholarship funds for farm children, widows' and orphans' pensions, group insurance, etc. Funds could even be invested in secondary processing plants with shares distributed to the farmers. Even a simple division of board proceeds on the basis of one-man-one-share would be desirable if the only other alternative is division of the board's share on a basis proportional to output. Indeed, a pure lottery would serve as well.

Even so, such options may not be completely accepted by farmers. Hence, as a second best approach the board would return wealth to individual farmers in some positive relationship to their output, <u>as long as the correlation between transfer and output is not unity</u>. Obviously, the closer the correlation between output and board transfer is to zero, the more will be the desirable effects on output, price, and profit of a given 1—r. The closer the correlation is to unity, the more damped will be the desired effects of a given tax rate.

The problem of correlating transfer with output could be illustrated with reference to Canada Wheat Board pricing and payments policy for prairie grain. The Canada Wheat Board not only pays a guaranteed "initial payment," to grain producers in the Prairie Provinces but has institutionalized the payment of "second" and even "third" payments as a means of distributing surplus from wheat sales. The subsequent, as well as initial, payments are made on the basis of a price per bushel of grain delivered, and are directly correlated by farmers with units sold. Uncertainty has tended to shift away from the question of whether or not second, third, or subsequent payments would be made at all, to how much per unit the second payment will be. As a result, the price per bushel used in the grain grower's production decision tends not to be the initial payment, but the initial payment plus an expected bonus per bushel. This expectation, over and above the initial payment, has been sufficient to encourage production well in excess of an ongoing expected sales flow. In fact it has only been the random occurrence of crop failure in other nations that has kept the Canadian wheat economy from bankruptcy.

This discussion indicates the need for some uncertainty in the distribution of "surplus" occurring from a negative supply management program, and uncertainty may be more attainable if surplus is not distributed in direct relation to output. The experience of the Canada Wheat Board has been cited here as a case in which fewer uncertainties, or rather uncertainties only surrounding the levels of bonus, exist. More uncertainty would be created if the return of bonuses to the farm sector were not made in proportion to sales levels.

Programs to Implement the Policy. The programs to implement negative supply management incorporating the essential elements as outlined above could be as simple as requesting, or enforcing through legislation or regulation, that existing marketing boards (1) restrict marketings only to attain price stability, not price improvement; (2) collect "check-off" fees proportional to the individual's output, after estimating how high these fees or taxes should be to attain a target price level; (3) abandon production or delivery quotas as a means of restricting entry and participation in production and altering the tax or fee structure to attain the same desired level of output; (4) redistribute the benefits from the supply restriction in a manner consistent with producers' needs, not necessarily their output; and (5) incorporate randomness in this redistribution.

Delivery quotas might still serve a purpose if this were deemed to be the best means of allocating scarce storage space fairly among producers. But once quotas ceased to be an integral part of some income support or distribution scheme, they could be viewed as one of many potential means of regulating product flow and would have their value judged in that light alone. It would be an important rationalizing step if boards used traditional instruments for attaining goals that could be attained with the instrument without creating harmful side effects (as is done now, when quotas become a part of a farm's fixed assets, and take on income "value").

Since much of the machinery for successful negative supply management (successful in the sense of rationalizing supply to existing and more or less inalterable demand) would already exist in the producer-managed marketing boards of today, it would seem best for them to change their roles slightly to make negative supply management work rather than to construct a new set of boards. With farm family income buttressed by programs to stabilize income directly, and apart from price levels, the more traditional role of marketing boards would become redundant. (It has already been shown that the traditional practices of marketing boards would not generally serve the income improvement and stabilization desires of farmers anyway.) Producer boards could give farmers the means of participating in the political activity of policy making, which further favors their retention. This would have the second benefit of forestalling suggestions that more superstructure be added to the Canadian institutional framework.

However, government should be prepared to follow other programs of negative supply management if existing producer marketing boards were not receptive to the proposed change in roles. The elements of successful negative supply management for the stabilization of price, the satisfaction of changing demands, and the minimization of the cost of direct income support programs could just as easily be incorporated in new legislation for new government-operated compulsory marketing boards. In this case, traditional marketing boards would be redundant and would soon die out. They could also be legislated out of existence. The economics of the situation might even suggest that a government body would be superior to a producer-operated board, for with government management, decisions as to the level of the tax, $1-r$, and the means of redistributing surplus income could be made with the object of optimizing with primary respect to national objectives. On the other hand, by permitting producer-operated boards to make these decisions, government would be permitting producers to optimize, giving primary concern to their own collective objectives, a process which does not guarantee the attainment of national objectives. Clearly, political power is shifting toward urban, or at least nonagricultural, bases, so that decisions optimizing national goal attainment would tend to rise in importance relative to those maximizing the welfare of special interest groups, if a conflict arises. Nonetheless it would still appear to be a least-cost, and hence better, choice to try and change the role of existing marketing boards first.

Consequently we do not offer a specific program for implementation of a negative supply management policy. No new policy-implementing structures need be constructed if the existing structures would adapt to new logic and new practices. In fact, this latter suggestion—that old institutions play new roles—poses a supreme challenge to existing farm-block leadership. Hopefully there are those in this leadership corps who are equal to the challenge.

CONCLUSION

This chapter has outlined a philosophy of supply management that is consistent with the programs suggested earlier for facilitating recurring adjustment in commercial agriculture, since the elements of positive and negative supply management given would tend to minimize the cost of income maintenance programs. It is a change from the traditional management approach, however, in that it avoids the use of quotas. Quotas were shown in Chapter 2 to have characteristics which would retard adjustment, even though supply withholding (negative supply management) could potentially add to agriculture's aggregate welfare.

Varying policy objectives of government or producer-elected boards could be achieved through the systems outlined here, including selected regional development goals using positive management, income goals for lower (but not poverty) income farmers who are still commercial, and general income stabilization, to minimize the costs of the income maintenance programs suggested earlier. None of this would be possible under the traditional method of quota manipulation.

A Estimating the Numbers of Commercial and Non-commercial Farms by 1981

IN ORDER to estimate the possible cost of the programs suggested in the text, an estimate of the number of farm families in 1971 is made, along with an estimate of the natural attrition rate anticipated over the 1970s. It is assumed for this calculation that one farm has one farm family and one operator, as defined by census. Farms with sales between $50 and $249 per annum are excluded, since they are either pure welfare cases or not seriously engaged in agricultural production.

The basis for this estimation is the Census of Agriculture for 1961 and 1966, and a study in which farm numbers were forecast in Ontario to 1971 and 1981.[1] The Ontario forecasts were made based on several suggested and verified hypotheses concerning the economic behavior of farm operators of varying ages on farms generating different levels of cash receipts.

PROCEDURE

It would be desirable to have estimates of the numbers of Canadian farms in 1971 cross-classified by economic class (receipts for agricultural products) and age of the operator. At the time of writing, the 1971 Census of Agriculture was not available; therefore, tabulations of census farms by economic class in 1961 and 1966 for Canada must serve (Table A1).

A linear extrapolation of the change of relative importance of each economic class is used to estimate the percentage distribution of census farms in 1971

1. R. W. Crown, Forecasting Farm Labour Employment in Ontario to 1981 (M. Sc. thesis; Univ. of Guelph, Guelph, Ontario, 1968), pp. 11-28.

Table A1. Farms by Economic Class—1961, 1966, and Estimate for 1971

Gross Sales ($)	1961[a] Number (000s) (1)	Percentage (2)	1966[a] Number (000s) (3)	Percentage (4)	1971 (est) Number (000s) (5)	Percentage[b] (6)
15,000+	23.9	5.5	50.8	12.9	68.4	20.4
10,000-14,999	25.9	5.9	44.2	11.2	55.5	16.6
5,000-9,999	90.4	20.7	96.9	24.7	95.9	28.6
250-4,999	296.0	67.9	201.2	51.2	115.8	34.5
Total	436.2[c]	100.0	393.1[c]	100.0	335.6[d]	100.0

[a]From Dominion Bureau of Statistics, Census of Agriculture 1961 and 1966, Ottawa.
[b]Linear extrapolation of col. 4 and col. 2.
[c]Part-time farms excluded.
[d]Represents 100 percent of Canadian farm numbers if Ontario accounts for 25.5 percent of Canadian total. See R. W. Crown, Forecasting Farm Labour Employment in Ontario to 1981 (M. Sc. thesis; Univ. of Guelph, Guelph, Ontario, 1968).

(col. 6 in Table A1). This extrapolation subsumes such changes as gross exit and gross entry into agriculture at different income levels between 1966 and 1971, upward and downward mobility between economic classes during the same period, and changes in interregional farm distribution. It is assumed that the economic forces causing the decline in the total number of Canadian farms over the 1961-66 period would continue to influence agricultural adjustment over the 1966-71 period in the same way. Lastly, since the value of money declined over the 1961-66 period, but the economic classes were not redefined in 1966 to take account of this, the forecasts are made, assuming that the value of money would decline between 1966 and 1971 at the same rate as it had from 1961 to 1966.

It was observed from census data that Ontario farms accounted for 25.14 percent of all Canadian census farms in 1961 and 25.31 percent of all Canadian census farms in 1966. It is thus assumed that in 1971 Ontario would account for 25.5 percent of all census farms. Therefore, given that the estimate of the number of farms in Ontario in 1971 is 85.5 thousand, with the age and economic cross-classification as detailed in

Table A2,[2] the estimated total number of farms in Canada in 1971 is 336 thousand. (A linear extrapolation of the trend in farm numbers between 1961 and 1966 would give an estimate of 350 thousand farms in 1971. The estimate in Table A1 is made to appear even more reasonable when one observes that the rate of decline between 1961 and 1966 is twice the rate of decline over the decade 1951-61 for the same economic classes. The decline in farm numbers is proceeding at an increasing rate, which makes the linear extrapolation of 1961 and 1966 observations to 1971 an overestimating procedure. See also footnote 4.)

The numbers of farms in each economic class in Table A1 for 1971 are estimated by multiplying the appropriate percentages by the estimate of the number of farms. By assuming that the age distribution of farm operators in Ontario is representative of Canadian farm operators generally, we subdivide the projected number of farms in each economic class according to the ages of the operators. This distribution is given in Table A3.

The assumption appears reasonable in that there are not likely to be economic forces operating in Ontario that do not affect all agriculture as a sector in Canada's national economy. One might argue that the inclusion of the Toronto-Hamilton-Oshawa industrial and business complex would tend to bias the age distribution upward, because of greater chances of successful out-migration among younger farmers. On the other hand, one would have to recognize that the availability of general markets for the entire cross section of agricultural products in the same urban complex could make farming profitable—a countervailing force. Unlike any other region, Ontario can be viewed as a national economy in the small and its agricultural sector presumed to be representative of a national agriculture.

COMMERCIAL AND NONCOMMERCIAL FARMS

Table A3 can be partitioned on the broken line to show the number of farms likely to fall into the classes defined as commercial farms in Chapter 5.

---

2. Ibid., p. 19.

Table A2. Ontario Farms, Estimated for 1971 by Economic Class and Age of Operators

Gross Sales ($)	(Age 15-24) (1)	Percentage of Class (2)	(Age 25-34) (3)	Percentage of Class (4)	(Age 35-44) (5)	Percentage of Class (6)	(Age 45-54) (7)	Percentage of Class (8)	(Age 55+) (9)	Percentage of Class (10)	Total in Class (11)
15,000+	239	1.60	1,993	13.41	4,136	27.84	4,354	29.31	4,131	27.81	14,853
10,000-14,999	143	1.33	1,306	12.13	2,899	26.83	3,255	30.24	3,158	29.34	10,761
5,000-9,999	287	1.28	2,669	11.95	5,378	24.08	6,562	29.39	7,430	33.27	22,326
250-4,999	509	1.35	2,903	7.73	5,800	15.45	9,166	24.42	19,150	51.02	37,528
Total	1,178	1.37	8,871	10.37	18,213	21.30	23,337	27.30	33,869	39.63	85,468

Source: R. W. Crown, Forecasting Farm Labour Employment in Ontario to 1981 (M. Sc. thesis; Univ. of Guelph, Guelph, Ontario, 1968), p. 19.

Table A3. Canadian Farms, Estimated for 1971 by Economic Class and Age of Operator

Gross Sales ($)	Age[a] 15-24 (000s)	25-34 (000s)	35-44 (000s)	45-54 (000s)	55+ (000s)	Total in Class[b] (000s)
15,000+	1.1	9.2	19.0	20.0	19.0	68.4
10,000-14,999	0.7	6.7	14.9	16.8	16.3	55.5
5,000-9,999	1.2	11.5	23.1	28.2	31.2	95.9
250-4,999	1.6	9.0	17.9	28.3	59.1	115.8
Total	4.6	36.3	74.9	93.3	126.3	335.6

[a]Percentages taken from Table A2.
[b]Table A1, col. 5.

Clearly, all those in economic classes $15,000+ and $10,000-$14,999 are commercial farms in that significant numbers of them would be in agriculture in 1981 even if no policy changes were made. Hence, there are at least 124 thousand commercial farms.

On the second partition, there are potentially 36 thousand in the $5,000-$9,999 economic class of operators under 45 years of age. But to enjoy continued viability, each of the farms involved would undoubtedly have to grow within the sector. What is the likelihood of this? We will assume that these also are commercial, giving an upward bias to the estimates of costs based on these farm number estimates.

The farms enumerated in the lower partition are the noncommercial farms. Significant numbers of these would leave agriculture even if no special program were designed to facilitate their withdrawal; they would withdraw in spite of government programs designed to keep them in production. Thus there would initially be about 176 thousand noncommercial farm operators, of which no more than 28 thousand could be expected—if only because of the ages—to leave the sector entirely. The remaining 138 thousand—those 45 and older in the two lowest economic classes—would take the position of retired or semiretired farmers in agriculture.

PROSPECTS FOR CHANGE BY 1981 WITH NO POLICY CHANGES

Based on the assumption that government policy would proceed in the same qualitative and relative

Table A4. Estimated Percentage Net Change in Ontario Farm Numbers 1971-81, by Economic Class and Age of Operator

Gross Sales ($)	Age Class (%) (15-24)	(25-34)	(35-44)	(45-54)	(55+)	Total in Class (%)
15,000+	−21.5	−16.6	−11.9	+12.3	+33.6	+ 7.1
10,000-14,999	−22.4	−21.1	−17.6	+ 4.4	+24.8	+ 1.1
5,000-9,999	−31.5	−28.4	−24.0	−15.6	− 1.7	−14.7
250-4,999	−68.6	−74.4	−75.2	−68.7	−41.8	−56.5
Total	−44.2	−40.1	−36.5	−28.5	−17.5	−27.3

Source: R. W. Crown, Forecasting Farm Labour Employment in Ontario to 1981 (M. Sc. thesis; Univ. of Guelph, Guelph, Ontario, 1968). Estimated by dividing 1981 entry by corresponding 1971 entry.

quantitative paths to 1981 as it has between 1951 and 1971, the study in Ontario can predict rates of change in numbers of farmers for farms by economic class and operator age classes.[3] These are given in Table A4.

The natural attrition rate indicated here is higher than that suggested elsewhere.[4] As a result, the estimate of farm numbers in 1981 is lower by about 15 percent than has otherwise been suggested.

3. Ibid., Table 2.1. The 1981 entry is divided by the corresponding 1971 entry.

4. See G. R. Purnell and V. A. Heighton, The Agricultural Situation in Canada in Can. Farm Econ., December 1970, Canadian Dept. of Agr., pp. 1-15, especially p. 10. These authors assume that the total number of farms would decline at an average annual rate of 2.6 percent.

B Description and Implications of Alternative Land Retirement Programs

THE EXISTENCE of the Lower Inventories for Tomorrow (LIFT) Program for land retirement in the Canadian Prairie Provinces and the possibilities that such programs may become widespread and perpetuated in Canada calls for some comments on land retirement programs in general.

There are various means of applying land withdrawal programs. These several alternatives differ in (1) their costs in attaining a given output reduction and price improvement, (2) their total treasury costs, (3) the amount of labor withdrawn from agriculture in conjunction with the land, and (4) the extent of the community adjustment problem created. Of course if programs are aimed at lessening acreage and output of a particular commodity such as wheat, restraints on other grains which compete for acreage in the same area must be applied. Otherwise the competing grains will simply take over the land retired from wheat production. The effects on total grain output would be entirely or largely negated, and the burden of adjustment would fall on those growing the competing grain. Since surplus capacity and competition in grain production is so prevalent in Canadian agriculture, it would make little sense to restrict acreage of one grain and not the other. Because of this interrelationship, it is unrealistic to apply market quotas on the output side or land restraints on the input side for one grain without doing it for other closely related

The helpful participation of Kenneth J. Nicol (M. Sc., University of Alberta) in preparing this appendix is acknowledged.

or competitive grains. The argument applies equally well to competing regions: all must be included, as transshipment of grain would defeat the action's intent.

PARTIAL RETIREMENT BY FARMS AND REGIONS

In this method of retiring land, all farmers in each region would be allowed to retire part of their land from the production of each major grain commodity. To participate they would enter into an annual contract with the government and would be given direct cash payments in much the same way as they would if they rented the land to the government—what they actually are doing. An upper limit would exist on the amount of land a farmer can be paid for withdrawing from the production of a given crop. Ordinarily he would not be permitted to use it for other purposes. When it is declared eligible for other uses, it would be restricted to grazing, a practice which causes some substitution of forage for feed grain.

The advantage of this system is that it would distribute cash payments among all farmers who wish to participate and would spread land withdrawal over many or most rural communities where field crop production is important. As only a fractional part of each farm is retired under this type of program, farm families would generally remain on their units and cultivate the remainder of the farm. Such a program would discourage an even heavier exodus of farm families from the land than already exists; therefore it would not add to the rural community problems brought about by labor-saving farm technology, loss of sales volume, depopulation, etc. The method also provides flexibility if demand and yields fluctuate considerably from year to year, since the withdrawal contracts would be on an annual basis. Hence the amount of idle land could be varied from year to year to maintain a desired carryover.

Compared to other means of supply control, and certainly when compared to other, more direct methods of improving farm income, this supply control mechanism has serious disadvantages. Spread over all farms and communities, it would cost more than alternative land withdrawal methods to attain given levels of supply control and price improvement. Farmers would have to be paid in proportion to the profit margin under every soil and climatic condition if all are to be encouraged to participate.

The per acre profit margin in highly productive locations exceeds that in less productive locations by a greater proportion than do yields. This follows from the realization that the basic per acre costs of operation, aside from fertilization and harvesting costs, exist for all land regardless of yield. Thus land which yields less has a lower margin between value of crop and production costs. Usually the farmer would only need a payment equal to the amount of the profit margin or a slight variation therefrom to be encouraged to idle his land. Hence, if all reduction were attained on less productive land, the same output restraint could be attained at a lower cost.

As an illustration of these points, we consider the land retirement program currently used in the United States. There the partial farm retirement program was set up in such a way that a maximum proportion of the "base acres" (wheat, feed grains, or total cultivated land) on a given farm could be withdrawn from production in which the farm operates. This means that a given region has an effective upper limit to the amount of land that can be retired within its boundaries.

The costs and benefits of alternative regional diversion levels have been evaluated for the United States agricultural sector. An Iowa State University study examines the cost of land withdrawal under diversion policies of unlimited regional withdrawal, with a maximum of 75 percent diversion in any region, 50 percent diversion in any region, and 25 percent diversion in any region.[1] Using a price level which approximates 1969 prices as a target to be maintained, government costs are estimated for each alternate division scheme. The costs (outlays as "rent" for land owned by farmers) range from $1.6 billion under the unlimited diversion program (unlimited amounts of land

1. Howard C. Madsen, Earl O. Heady, and Kenneth J. Nicol, Trade-Offs in Farm Policy, CARD Report 36, Iowa State University, 1970.

could be withdrawn from any region), to $1.8 billion under the program with a maximum of 25 percent diversion in a region.[2] The study shows that, as restrictions on land retirement increase, the distribution of retired acres moves from the less productive to the more productive areas. As the less productive land remains in production, fewer acres of the more productive land are retired to maintain the desired output. However, due to productive efficiency, the more productive land requires a larger payment per acre not farmed, and the total cost of the program increases. This suggests that in a land retirement program government should consider concentrating its efforts on removing less profitable land first, regardless of the fact that it implies the full retirement of entire farm units in some regions.

Another disadvantage of the system, in addition to the annual cost aspect, is the fact that only a fraction of the farm is idled. The farmer thus would reduce the utilization of labor and equipment which would usually be retained as unused capacity and not scrapped. Hence, as soon as the program is lifted, he would immediately plough up the idled land and put it back into use in order to more fully employ his labor and capital. Too, when the program is on an annual basis, the farmer's expectations would be similar, and he would not make long-run shifts in land use, for example, convert it to forestry or grazing. Finally, the proportion of land withdrawal has to be considerably greater than the proportion of reduced output to be attained. One reason is that farmers idle their least productive land and retain that with higher yields. Also, the capital formerly employed on the idled land, the direct payments received as rent, and labor input can be used for a more intensive operation of the land remaining in production. Thus over time this type of program would require increased outlays, since "last year's" profit on the acres tilled would be the basis on which "this year's" rental arrangement is made. For these reasons, programs like Canada's recent LIFT Program to retire acreage in the Prairie Provinces during

2. Ibid., p. 33.

1970 are completely inadequate to solve the capacity problem at least cost.

FULL-FARM RETIREMENT IN ANY REGION

An alternative method of land withdrawal would be payment for the retirement of entire farms. This methof was used quite widely under the Conservation Reserve Program in the United States. It is currently used on a very limited scale under the Cropland Adjustment Program.

The advantage of the program would be that it idles both good and poor land on single farms, and removes all the capital equipment and labor of the farm from production. However, the system also has the effect of encouraging greater migration of labor from farms.

Such land withdrawal could be attained at a lower cost than under the system previously outlined because the farmer is relieved of some of his fixed costs, as well as the fixed per acre operating costs. (As one of the alternatives, the Iowa State University study discusses unlimited land withdrawal by region. This program gives the lowest direct government payment to farmers, although no compensation is made to nonfarm members of the community for losses suffered to the smaller population base. In the programs of Chap. 7, however, this shortcoming would be overcome.) The farmer would no longer need an investment in equipment and machinery with associated costs in depreciation, taxes, and interest. He would not cultivate the remaining acres and so would be free to take nonfarm employment. Therefore, he would not need as large a cash payment as an inducement to retire his land as when he stayed on the farm and it was his sole source of income.

FULL-FARM RETIREMENT BY SELECTED INDIVIDUAL REGIONS

A third means of land retirement for purposes of supply control and price stabilization could be the retirement of entire farms concentrated in regions of marginal soils with low and variable yields. No attempt would be made to retire land in regions where land is most productive and yields are stable. This method has an even lower cost in the future of attaining ongoing stable levels of supply and price if the program is (1) voluntary, and farmers are offered prices that encourage complete withdrawal, or (2) mandatory, at an equitable price, where yields are lowest and the program objective is to withdraw land at the lowest equitable cost.

The method has all the advantages listed above for whole farm retirement in any region. As noted, too, the regional concentration of land withdrawal contributed to lowering the costs of supply control. The system has advantages if a long-run land use rationalization is to be made, surplus capacity exists, and farmers are to be given concentrated aid in making the shift to noncrop uses of land.

As compared to those outlined above, this method of land withdrawal would have the disadvantage of concentrating the costs of adjustment in restraining supply capacity to communities where the shift must be made. Farmers themselves in these regions would not, or need not, sacrifice, because the payments for participation could leave them better off than previously, particularly if they move to nonfarm jobs. A burden would fall, however, on other members of the rural community. Since labor and capital use would be all but eliminated through whole farm retirement, many farm families can be expected to migrate to other occupations, which are seldom available in the local farm community. Consequently the community would suffer a more rapid reduction in population than normal. This in turn would lower the volume of sales and income of local business establishments, reduce the number of people available for community activities, and even lower the tax base. Even so, with the added features of Programs 4, 5, and 6 in Chapter 6, these costs to the community could be minimized.

If a program of this type were to be considered as a supply control mechanism, it would be best "phased in" over a five-to-ten-year period. This rate of change could be acceptable to the community, since time would exist for least-cost adjustment. The amount of land which could be retired in any one year could possibly be no more than 20 percent of the total farm area in a five-year program, and 10 percent in a ten-year period. Such a land retirement program should be pursued in conjunction with a system of community aid policies, because whole farm and regional retirement programs create very serious hardships for those nonfarm families in the rural community who depend on the surrounding farmers for their income. In the case of regional concentration of land retirement, the retraining programs and often migration assistance described in Program 6 should be available for nonfarm populations of the adjusting regions or communities, as well as the farm population.

THE USE OF COMPETITIVE BIDDING

Regardless of the type of land retirement system used for supply control and price stabilization, its cost will be minimized if farmers are allowed, or required, to "bid" on the withdrawal of their land.[3] The bids accepted by public authority, if cost minimization is an objective of supply control, would be those which, considering crop yields, would give the largest amount of output reduction per dollar for participation. Hence, a normal, or average, yield would be established for each farmer who offers his land for retirement. Essentially, a supply function exists for land for retirement, just as it exists for any other commodity. The authority administering such a program would first acquire the land representing the largest potential production, then acquire the next most productive, and so forth, until the desired level of production reduction is attained.

ANNUAL PUBLIC RENTING

Any of the above systems could operate as annual programs. Contracts could be made for one year during

3. The retirement programs examined in Madsen, Heady, and Nicol, Trade-Offs in Farm Policy, were all based on farmers withdrawing their land at a cost to the government equivalent to their expected return. Thus any farmer who can receive this amount plus some dollar amount for maintaining the land should be willing to retire his land from production. With this pricing system, the total cost would be less than paying all farmers the marginal cost of the last acre retired.

which the public "rents" the land from the farmer for purposes of nonuse. Annual programs do have the advantage of flexibility. The public is committed only to a single-year rental and the program can be terminated at any time. Or, if there are unanticipated decreases or increases in yields, the program could be temporarily enlarged or contracted.

The disadvantage of an annual program includes its greater dollar costs. If there are legal and political possibilities that the program could be terminated or reformulated at the year's end, some farmers will refuse to participate because of greater certainty in continued production, regardless of prices, than in interrupted production. It also discourages families from moving to other occupations and locations. They tend to stay near agriculture so that they could return to the farm the next year if the program is terminated. The land stands ready to be returned to production at the end of any year by the former owner or a neighboring operator, and hence long-run shifts of land to other uses are discouraged. Thus annual schemes do not encourage more desirable use of land, only prevent current uses.

PUBLIC PURCHASE OF LAND

At the other extreme is outright public purchase of the land so it can be permanently shifted to other uses. For the reasons mentioned above, the annual cost of such a program would be less than any with annual renting. However, if surplus capacity is large, and it is expected that a supply control program would be needed far into the future, experience in the United States has shown that the difference in costs of the two programs can be tremendous.

Currently, the United States has a "rent land out of production" policy for which it has made annual payments over most of the last four decades. It has been calculated that the cost of such annual programs over that period has been more than enough to cover the cost of public purchase of all cropland in the nation at an average price for the period. Had the United States bought sufficient land to curtail production with a price level in mind, it would not be locked into perpetual annual payments to remove land from production now. In spite of the vast expenditures, the rental program has not solved the problem of surplus capacity. More disturbing and frustrating is the fact that annual payments must continue and grow in volume far into the future if the same method is to be used as a means of bolstering farm prices and incomes.

Included in the series of studies on farm policies at Iowa State University was an analysis of long-term land purchase alternatives. A hypothetical program was designed to withdraw sufficient cropland from production to maintain a desired price level under a free market system. The land was to be withdrawn on a whole farm basis, necessitating the removal of 103 million acres. The total cost of the program would have been $19 billion compared to the $3.1 billion paid for government land retirement and price support programs in 1967.[4] The withdrawal would have to occur over time as farmers become willing to sell their farms; thus a decreasing annual rental program would have to accompany the purchase program in the initial years.

Judged from a decade-long viewpoint, however, the program to purchase would still cost about $19 billion, and annual renting would have cost $31 billion—a similar situation to that described in Chapter 6. If the program of purchase had included resale or lease-back provisions (as the proposed scheme in Chap. 6 does), the decade-long cost would have been considerably less than the $19 billion. The program would have been cost competitive with even the "bid base" program, costing $18 billion over ten years.[5]

With technical progress likely in the future, Canada has prospects of a greater surplus acreage if commodity prices of the past decade are to be maintained. Not only can public land purchase cost less if

---

4. Earl O. Heady, Howard C. Madsen, and Leo V. Mayer, Analysis of Some Farm Program Alternatives for the Future, CAED Report 34, Iowa State University, Ames, 1969, pp. 11, 22.

5. Madsen, Heady, and Nicol, Trade-Offs in Farm Policy, p. 33.

the problem of surplus is chronic, but also the public has the control and investment opportunity of shifting the land to other uses.

There are disadvantages to the system. Land purchase requires a larger public fund in initial stages since the capitalized value of the land, rather than the annual rental price, is involved. But even here, if the government paid for its land on an amortized basis, little more than "down payments" would be required initially, with payments made annually in the way that current supports are paid.

EASEMENTS AND RIGHTS PURCHASE

A less complex and lower cost method which also permits a single outlay for continuous production control, in contrast to annual rental or outright purchase, would involve public purchase of the "rights" of farmers to produce crops for which surplus capacity exists. The farmer would only sell his rights to produce those crops while retaining ownership and the right to produce any other crops. He would be free to make his own management and investment decisions except that he could not produce any of the controlled crops. The program, as outlined earlier for land retirement programs generally, would be on a bid basis if a least-cost method is an objective. It could also be spread over a period of five years so that adjustment need not fall too rapidly and heavily on the nonfarm sector of the rural community. On a bid basis, it could be expected that, over time, the land withdrawal would concentrate on marginal lands and in the least productive and more unstable soil areas. The United States Conservation Reserve Program operated on a bid basis with contracts for ten years, to the extent allowed by law. A limit was placed on the amount of cropland which could be withdrawn under the program in each county. However, as much as a third of all cropland in some large producing areas went into the program. Again, this public ownership of rights is permanent, so that land changing hands would do so with this lien in force.

An alternative to the bidding system would be for

the public to use its legal powers to acquire easements on farms to be shifted out of crop production. The public would acquire and hold the right to produce surplus crops, this right being withdrawn from the farmer. The farmer would be free to use his resources for any noncontrol crops.

Either system would require some capital investments on the part of farmers shifting from field crops to forage and grazing or forestry. Farming would be less intensive, requiring larger units and fewer farms. Hence the adjustment facilitating programs of Chapter 7 would still be required.

Either method would cost less than outright public purchase because the farmer could still produce noncontrol crops. Public management and administrative costs would be minimized since farmers would still operate the land and make decisions within these cropping restraints. Programs would emphasize the shift of land from crops with surplus prospects to improved uses consistent with market conditions. Either method also would cost less than rental on the basis of annual contracts over a long period.

The Iowa State University studies consider two forms of the easement approach to land retirement.[6] Initially the study considers removing the right to produce all commodities and then relaxes this restriction and allows for the transfer of cropland to pasture. Government costs under the first alternative reach $1.4 billion, but these payments do not include any money for compensation or retraining programs for the rural nonfarm population displaced or penalized by the reduction of farming in the area. The second phase of the study allows for the production of beef on either 50 percent of the diverted land or alternatively on all diverted land. This practice increases the output of beef from 28 million pounds to 36 million pounds when all diverted land is used and causes a decline in the price of beef from 22 cents per pound to 16.3 cents per pound. The government cost of this type

6. Heady, Madsen, and Mayer, Farm Program Alternatives, pp. 4, 22-32, 36-41.

of program ranges from $0.9 billion under the unlimited retirement and maximum of 50 percent of the retired land used for beef, to $1.3 billion with a restricted land retirement program and unlimited use of the retired land for beef production. The use of beef as an alternative on the retired cropland reduces the government payments by the per acre profit received from beef production in the area. As beef production increases, the land used is less productive, and beef production contributes less to the rental of the land. The expanded production of beef also reduces the price of beef, decreasing the income to help cover the rent on the more productive land, causing government payments to increase as the amount of beef produced increases.

Any program which allows for the substitution of alternate crop or livestock production in place of the regulated activity must consider the possible effect on the substitute enterprise. Beef prices in the above example could be forced down to where the beef industry would require support programs, or if another crop is substituted, the prices of this crop would then be reduced and require price support programs. Other long-run alternatives which should be considered for a program include the development of forested areas or parkland development. The latter would ease the adjustment for the nonfarm members of the community as well as provide employment opportunities for some of the farmers who participate in the program.

It may be argued that the main disadvantage of such long-term land retirement systems is their lack of flexibility. Presumably, as opponents might suggest, adjustment could not be made for any rapid change in the world food supply or demand as quickly as under annual programs. The potential for production on existing acreages to respond to minute changes in price through more intensive capital application, and the existence of positive supply management programs outlined in Chapter 8 will probably prevent such land shortages from materializing.

INDEX